Best Ninja Foodi Dual Zone Air Fryer Cookbook UK

Ninja Air Fryer Recipes For Breakfast, Lunch, Dinner And Dessert That Prove The Do-It-All Appliance Can't Be Beat

JASMINE KERR

TABLE OF CONTENT

INTRODUCTION

Among the many air fryers that top the chart for kitchen appliances, Ninja® Foodi® 6-In-1 8-Qt. 2-Basket Air Fryer with Dual ZONE™ Technology has a notable reputation. Equipped with the patented dual-ZONE technology, this air fryer comes with two drawers. It has broken the barriers to cooking and has an unconventional design and feature. With two drawers and dual-ZONE technology, you can make two separate dishes in a selected timeframe easily. Thus, no more waiting for back-to-back cooking! Furthermore, this also makes it a fantastic air fryer in which you can cook large batches. Moreover, this air fryer has six amazing features that make cooking super easy for you.

This cookbook aims to give you a detailed insight into not just the recipes you can make in this air fryer but also its functions, maintenance, and cleaning. Throughout the chapters of this cookbook, you will get detailed information on each function of this air fryer, how you can use it, and lastly, how to maintain and keep it clean.

Lastly, you get 100 amazing recipes that will only make your life in the kitchen easier. So, what are you waiting for? Read ahead for everything you need to know about Ninja® Foodi® 6-In-1 8-Qt. 2-Basket Air Fryer with DualZONE™ Technology.

ESSENTIALS OF NINJA FOODI 2 BASKET AIR FRYER

1. Functions Of Ninja Foodi 2-Basket Air Fryer

Ninja dz201 foodi 2-basket air fryer is not just famous because of the dual basket technology, and there is so much more to it. It is so versatile that it can replace an oven, almost and even those expensive dehydrators. Of course, ninja has the best cooking technologies we have observed so far, and the ninja foodi 2-basket air fryer comes with a handful of functions as well. Yes, you heard it right; there are the six functions in the ninja foodi 2-basket air fryer that will make your life easy:

Air fry

The air fry function lets you fry the food with that beautiful golden exterior with less oil. It is just perfect for french fries, fried chicken, fried calamari, and so much more. And here is a caught; you do not need to have a temperature thermometer, big pots, and excess oil that will probably go to waste.

Indeed, you can easily set the temperature for whatever you are frying according to its texture. Thus, frying was never that easy!

Air broil

Who doesn't love to have the melted cheese and the crispy broil exterior? Air broil function is here to crisp up, melt and brown the toppings of your dish in just a few minutes.

Air broiling is also perfect for many non-traditional broiling like crème brûlée and even a steak. Indeed, there are so many food options that do not require full-time baking, just a sear-like heat from the air fryer, and this function is so efficient.

ROAST

ROAST dinners are very hard to get suitable with consistent temperatures. Honestly, you can

ROAST multiple proteins and vegetables with the two drawers and ROAST function without waiting for one to be done first. It helps you ROAST the food according to their perfect temperature and without the aromas mingling! Thus, you get each element of your ROAST done in the quickest time possible.

BAKE

Baking in an air fryer may have some mixed reviews, but we think it is worth it. You can BAKE at the lowest temperatures and control the browning of the food according to your preference in an air fryer. And the best thing about using an air fryer for baking is that you do not need to wait for 10 minutes of preheating. Thus, it is quick and controlled.

Reheat

Reheating food may often take away the beautiful exterior of the food. Mostly, people face uneven heating too. But in ninja foodi 2-basket air fryer, the air regulates evenly throughout the basket, helping you reheating your premade food or leftovers without ruining the perfect textures you have already achieved.

Dehydrate

The dehydration process took the internet by storm, and there are so many things that you can turn into delicious snacks and even perverse with the help of the dehydration process. You may also have heard of using an oven as a dehydrator, but that is an excellent hustle because of the lower temperatures the process needs. Ninja foodi 2-basket air fryer is made to be a dehydrator for you and someone you have tried making dried apples and many snacks like this; there is no going back to store-bought items

How to Use Ninja Foodi 2 Basket Air Fryer?

First off, you will notice the touch-controlled panel over the air fryer, and that is where the magic starts. All of the six functions of the air fryer can easily be chosen and set for either one of the drawers or both.

But the only question stands is how you can use this magnificent yet beautiful beast for your food. Here is a complete and easy guide that will help you use each function in your ninja foodi 2 basket air fryer without any hustle:

Basic start-up

1.   Start the ninja foodi 2 basket air fryer by pressing "power" to switch it on.

2.   Select the basket you are cooking in by selecting "1" for the basket ZONE on the left or "2" for the basket ZONE on the right side.

AIR FRY

1.   After selecting the basket, press the button "air fry".

2.   Select the temperature by using the temperature arrows on the top left side, near the power button. The maximum temperature is 400 f, and the minimum is 300 f.

3.   Set the timer by using the arrows on the top right side near start/pause. The maximum time you can set is for an hour.

4.   Press the "start/pause" button on the right top corner to start the process.

AIR BROIL

1.   After selecting the basket, press the button "air broil".

2.   Select the temperature by using the temperature arrows on the top left side, near the power button. The maximum temperature is 450 f, and the minimum is 400 f.

3.   Set the timer by using the arrows on the top right side near start/pause. The maximum

time you can set is 30 minutes.

4.	Press the "start/pause" button on the right top corner to start the process.

Note: ZONE 1 or basket 1 is the only one that can broil. But you can always change it to other functions as well.

ROAST

1.	After selecting the basket, press the button "ROAST".

2.	Select the temperature by using the temperature arrows. The maximum temperature is 400 f, and the minimum is 250 f.

3.	Set the timer by using the arrows. The maximum time you can set is 4 hours.

4.	Press the "start/pause" button to start the process.

BAKE

1.	After selecting the basket, press the button "BAKE".

2.	Select the temperature by using the temperature arrows. The maximum temperature is 400 f, and the minimum is 250 f.

3.	Set the timer by using the arrows. The maximum time you can set is 4 hours.

REHEAT

1.	After selecting the basket, press the button "reheat".

2.	Select the temperature by using the temperature arrows. The maximum temperature is 400 f, and the minimum is 270 f.

3.	Set the timer by using the arrows. The maximum time you can set for an hour.

4.	Press the "start/pause" button to start the process.

DEHYDRATE

1.	After selecting the basket, press the button "dehydrate".

2.	Select the temperature by using the temperature arrows. The maximum temperature is 195 f, and the minimum is 105 f.

3.	Set the timer by using the arrows. The maximum time you can set for 12 hours.

4.	Press the "start/pause" button to start the process.

There are few other buttons that you will see over the control panel; let us review them as well and discuss how they work as well:

Smart finish

It sets the cooking time of both drawers to finish at the same time. In short, it syncs them for the food to be cooked simultaneously to serve them right away.

1.	Fill in both drawers with food.

2.	Start the air fryer with the "power" button.

3.	By default, it will select basket ZONE 1. Select the cooking function.

4.	Once done selecting the function, set the temperature and timer.

5.	Now press the "2" for basket ZONE 2. Select the cooking function for it as well.

6.	Set the temperature and timer for ZONE 2.

7.	Press "smart finish" in the middle left of the panel.

8.	Press the "start/pause" button to start cooking. You will notice the lesser time basket will be displaying "hold" on the screen. It will begin as soon as the other basket is left with the same time to complete.

Note: air boil function is not available for the smart finish function.

MATCH cooking

The MATCH cooking will apply the same cooking settings on both drawers to cook in large batches.

1.   Fill in both drawers with the same ingredients or food.

2.   Start the air fryer with the "power" button.

3.   By default, it will select basket ZONE 1. Select the cooking function.

4.   Once done selecting the function, set the temperature and timer.

5.   Press "MATCHing cook" in the middle right of the panel. You will notice the ZONE 2 is set to the same setting as ZONE 1 on the screen.

6.   Press the "start/pause" button to start cooking.

Note: air boil function is not available for the MATCH cooking function.

USING BOTH DRAWERS MANUALLY

You can still use both drawers at the same time with different temperatures and cooking times. Both will start at the same time but ends on the timer you have set. In short, it is opposite to what we were doing in "start finish".

1.   Fill in both drawers with food.

2.   Start the air fryer with the "power" button.

3.   By default, it will select basket ZONE 1. Select the cooking function.

4.   Once done selecting the function, set the temperature and timer.

5.   Now press the "2" for basket ZONE 2. Select the cooking function for it as well.

6.   Set the temperature and timer for ZONE 2.

7.   Press the "start/pause" button to start cooking. You will notice both drawers will start cooking together and finish at their own time.

MAINTAINING AND CLEANING

You have heard from many that cleaning an air fryer can be loads of work. One of the popular opinions is that you may regret cleaning in time. That is somehow true since once you have cooked in an air fryer. As soon as the drawers start to cool down, the residue from the food and fats sticks to the basket and harden up.

So, the first step of maintenance of the ninja foodi 2-basket air fryer is cleaning. Following are the steps that can help you clean the air fryer:

1.   Try to clean the air fryer as soon as you finish cooking or within an hour. The main reason is that the basket is still hot, and the residue has not settled.

2.   Carefully remove all components and clean them with warm water with soap. Try to use a cloth or soft sponge.

3.   Say no to abrasive. If something isn't removed from the basket, even warm water, try heating the basket with water and sliced lime. Let it sit until it cools, drain and clean with a towel.

4.   Clean the body and the insides of the air fryer with a damp cloth. Make sure that is it has cool down and unplug to avoid any mishap and electrocution.

5.   If the drawers or any component smells, heating them with water and limes will undoubtedly remove the smell.

BREAKFAST RECIPES

SAUSAGE WITH EGGS

 **PREPARATION TIME**
10 MINUTES

 **COOKING TIME**
12 MINUTES

 SERVINGS
2 PERSONS

INGREDIENTS:

- 4 sausage links, raw and uncooked
- 4 eggs, uncooked
- 1 tablespoon green onion
- 2 tablespoons chopped tomatoes
- Salt and black pepper, to taste
- 2 tablespoons milk, dairy
- Oil spray, for greasing

PREPARATIONS:

1. Whisk eggs to smooth in a bowl.
2. Add milk, and add onions and tomatoes.
3. Combine well.
4. Season with salt and black pepper.
5. Using the cooking spray, grease a cake pan that fits inside the air fryer with oil.
6. Pour the omelet into the greased cake pans.
7. Slice the sausages into round shapes and put them on eggs.
8. Select AIR FRY mode for 3 minutes at 325 degrees F to preheat the air fryer
9. Press START/PAUSE to start the preheating process.
10. Once preheating is done, put the cake pan inside the unit.
11. Press the Air Fry function of Ninja Air Fryer, and set the timer to 12 minutes at 310 degrees F.
12. Once the cooking cycle completes, serve by transferring it to plates.
13. Enjoy hot as a delicious breakfast.

Serving Suggestion: Serve it with toasted bread slices.

Variation Tip: Use almond milk if you like non-dairy milk.

Nutrition:

CALORIES 240 | FAT 18.4G| SODIUM 396MG | CARBS 2.8G | FIBER0.2G | SUGAR 2G | PROTEIN 15.6G

BREAKFAST BACON

 **PREPARATION TIME**
10 MINUTES

 **COOKING TIME**
14 MINUTES

 SERVINGS
4 PERSONS

INGREDIENTS:

- ½ lb. bacon slices

PREPARATIONS:

1. Preheat your Air Fryer to 390°F with the Air Fry mode.
2. Arrange the bacon slices in a single layer in the Air Fryer Basket.
3. Place the Air Fryer Basket back in the Air Fryer and cook for an additional 14 minutes.
4. Press the START/PAUSE BUTTON to begin cooking.
5. Once the crispy bacon is halfway done, flip it and continue cooking.
6. Serve.

Serving Suggestion: Serve the bacon with eggs and bread slices.

Variation Tip: Add salt and black pepper for seasoning.

Nutrition:

CALORIES 273 | FAT 22G |SODIUM 517MG | CARBS 3.3G | FIBER 0.2G | SUGAR 1.4G | PROTEIN 16.1G

PEPPER EGG CUPS

 **PREPARATION TIME**
15 MINUTES

 **COOKING TIME**
18 MINUTES

 SERVINGS
4 PERSONS

INGREDIENTS:

- 2 bell pepper, halved, seeds removed
- 4 eggs
- 1 teaspoon olive oil
- 1 pinch salt and black pepper
- 1 pinch sriracha flakes

PREPARATIONS:

1. Preheat your Air Fryer to 390°F using Air Fry mode.
2. 2. To make a cup-like form, cut the bell peppers in half lengthwise and remove the seeds and inside portion.
3. Brush the bell peppers' edges with olive oil.
4. Place them cut side up in the Air Fryer Basket and crack 1 egg into each half of bell pepper.
5. Season the eggs with salt, black pepper, and sriracha flakes.
6. Place the Air Fryer Basket back in the Air Fryer and cook for an additional 18 minutes.
7. Press the START/PAUSE BUTTON to begin cooking.
8. Serve warm and fresh.

Serving Suggestion: Serve the cups with toasted bread slices and crispy bacon.

Variation Tip: Broil the cups with mozzarella cheese on top.

Nutrition:

CALORIES 183 | FAT 15G |SODIUM 402MG | CARBS 2.5G | FIBER 0.4G | SUGAR 1.1G | PROTEIN 10G

CRISPY HASH BROWNS

 **PREPARATION TIME**
10 MINUTES

 **COOKING TIME**
13 MINUTES

 SERVINGS
4 PERSONS

INGREDIENTS:

- 3 russet potatoes
- ¼ cup chopped green peppers
- ¼ cup chopped red peppers
- ¼ cup chopped onions
- 2 garlic cloves chopped
- 1 teaspoon paprika
- Salt and black pepper, to taste
- 2 teaspoons olive oil

PREPARATIONS:

1. Preheat your Air Fryer to 390°F using Air Fry mode.
2. Using a cheese grater, peel and grate all of the potatoes.
3. Soak potato shreds for 25 minutes in a bowl filled with cold water.
4. Drain the water and spread the potato shreds on a paper towel-lined dish.
5. Toss the shreds with olive oil, paprika, garlic, and black pepper in a dry basin.
6. Using the potato mixture, form four flat patties and place them in the Air Fryer Basket.
7. Place the Air Fryer Basket back in the Air Fryer and cook for an additional 13 minutes.
8. Press the START/PAUSE BUTTON to begin cooking.
9. Flip the potato hash browns once cooked halfway through, then resume cooking.
10. Once done, serve warm.

Serving Suggestion: Serve the hash with toasted bread slices and crispy bacon.

Variation Tip: Add herbed cream on top of the hash browns.

Nutrition:

CALORIES 190 | FAT 18G |SODIUM 150MG | CARBS 0.6G | FIBER 0.4G | SUGAR 0.4G | PROTEIN 7.2G

PUMPKIN MUFFINS

 **PREPARATION TIME**
15 MINUTES

 **COOKING TIME**
13 MINUTES

 SERVINGS
8 PERSONS

INGREDIENTS:

- ½ cup pumpkin puree
- 1 cup gluten-free oats
- ¼ cup honey
- 1 medium egg beaten
- ½ teaspoon coconut butter
- ½ tablespoons cocoa nib
- ½ tablespoons vanilla essence
- Cooking spray
- ½ teaspoon nutmeg

PREPARATIONS:

1. Preheat your Air Fryer to 390°F using Air Fry mode.
2. In a mixing dish, combine the oats, honey, eggs, pumpkin puree, coconut butter, chocolate nibs, vanilla essence, and nutmeg.
3. Pour the batter into a muffin tin that has been coated with cooking spray.
4. In the Air Fryer Basket, place the muffin tray.
5. Place the Air Fryer Basket back in the Air Fryer and cook for an additional 13 minutes.
6. Press the START/PAUSE BUTTON to begin cooking.
7. Allow the muffins to cool, then serve.

Serving Suggestion: Serve the muffins with hot coffee.
Variation Tip: Add raisins and nuts to the batter before baking.

Nutrition:

CALORIES 209 | FAT 7.5G |SODIUM 321MG | CARBS 34.1G | FIBER 4G | SUGAR 3.8G | PROTEIN 4.3G

CINNAMON TOASTS

 **PREPARATION TIME**
15 MINUTES

 **COOKING TIME**
8 MINUTES

 SERVINGS
4 PERSONS

INGREDIENTS:

- 4 pieces of bread
- 2 tablespoons butter
- 2 eggs, beaten
- 1 pinch salt
- 1 pinch cinnamon ground
- 1 pinch nutmeg ground
- 1 pinch ground clove
- 1 teaspoon icing sugar

PREPARATIONS:

1. Preheat your Air Fryer to 390°F using Air Fry mode.
2. In a mixing dish, whisk together two eggs, cinnamon, nutmeg, ground cloves, and salt.
3. Brush both sides of the bread pieces with butter and cut them into thick strips.
4. Place the breadsticks in the Air Fryer Basket after dipping them in the egg mixture.
5. Place the Air Fryer Basket back in the Air Fryer and cook for an additional 8 minutes.
6. Press the START/PAUSE BUTTON to begin cooking.
7. Flip the French toast sticks when cooked halfway through.
8. Serve.

Serving Suggestion: Serve the toasted with chocolate syrup or Nutella spread.

Variation Tip: Use crushed cornflakes for bread to have extra crispiness.

Nutrition:

CALORIES 199 | FAT 11.1G |SODIUM 297MG | CARBS 14.9G | FIBER 1G | SUGAR 2.5G | PROTEIN 9.9G

MORNING EGG ROLLS

PREPARATION TIME
15 MINUTES

COOKING TIME
13 MINUTES

SERVINGS
6 PERSONS

INGREDIENTS:

- 2 eggs
- 2 tablespoons milk
- Salt, to taste
- Black pepper, to taste
- ½ cup shredded cheddar cheese
- 2 sausage patties
- 6 egg roll wrappers
- 1 tablespoon olive oil
- 1 cup of water

PREPARATIONS:

1. Preheat your Air Fryer to 390°F using Air Fry mode.
2. Place a small skillet over medium heat, greased with olive oil.
3. Add sausage patties and cook them until brown.
4. Chop the cooked patties into small pieces. Beat eggs with salt, black pepper, and milk in a mixing bowl.
5. Grease the same skillet with 1 teaspoon of olive oil and pour the egg mixture into it.
6. Stir cook to make scrambled eggs.
7. Add sausage, mix well and remove the skillet from the heat.
8. Spread an egg roll wrapper on the working surface in a diamond shape position.
9. Add a tablespoon of cheese at the bottom third of the roll wrapper.
10. Top the cheese with an egg mixture and wet the edges of the wrapper with water.
11. Fold the two corners of the wrapper and roll it, then seal the edges.
12. Repeat the same steps and place the rolls in the Air Fryer Basket.
13. Place the Air Fryer Basket again in the Air Fryer and cook for 13 minutes.
14. Press the START/PAUSE BUTTON to begin cooking.
15. Flip the rolls after 8 minutes and continue cooking for another 5
16. minutes.
17. Serve warm and fresh.

Serving Suggestion: Serve the rolls with your favorite hot sauce or cheese dip.

Variation Tip: Add crispy bacon to the filling.

Nutrition:

CALORIES 282 | FAT 15G |SODIUM 526MG | CARBS 20G | FIBER 0.6G | SUGAR 3.3G | PROTEIN 16G

MORNING PATTIES

 **PREPARATION TIME**
15 MINUTES

 COOKING TIME
13 MINUTES

 SERVINGS
4 PERSONS

INGREDIENTS:

- 1 lb. minced pork
- 1 lb. minced turkey
- 2 teaspoons dry rubbed sage
- 2 teaspoons fennel seeds
- 2 teaspoons garlic powder
- 1 teaspoon paprika
- 1 teaspoon sea salt
- 1 teaspoon dried thyme

PREPARATIONS:

1. Preheat your Air Fryer to 390°F using Air Fry mode.
2. In a mixing bowl, add turkey and pork, then mix properly.
3. Mix sage, fennel, paprika, salt, thyme, and garlic powder in a small bowl.
4. Drizzle this mixture over the meat mixture and mix well.
5. Take 2 tablespoons of this mixture at a time and roll it into thick patties.
6. Spray the patties with cooking oil and place them in the Air Fryer Basket.
7. Place the Air Fryer Basket again in the Air Fryer and cook for 10 minutes.
8. Press the START/PAUSE BUTTON to begin cooking.
9. Flip the patties in the basket once cooked halfway through.
10. Serve warm and fresh.

Serving Suggestion: Serve the patties with toasted bread slices.

Variation Tip: Ground chicken or beef can also be used instead of ground pork and turkey.

Nutrition:

CALORIES 305 | FAT 25G |SODIUM 532MG | CARBS 2.3G | FIBER 0.4G | SUGAR 2G | PROTEIN 18.3G

BISCUIT BALLS

 **PREPARATION TIME**
10 MINUTES

 **COOKING TIME**
18 MINUTES

 SERVINGS
6 PERSONS

INGREDIENTS:

- 1 tablespoon butter
- 2 eggs, beaten
- ¼ teaspoon pepper
- 1 can (10.2-oz) Pillsbury Buttermilk biscuits
- 2 ounces cheddar cheese, diced into ten cubes
- Cooking spray
- Egg Wash
- 1 egg
- 1 tablespoon water

PREPARATIONS:

1. Preheat your Air Fryer to 390°F using Air Fry mode.
2. Place a suitable non-stick skillet over medium-high heat and cook the bacon until crispy, then place it on a plate lined with a paper towel.
3. Melt butter in the same skillet over medium heat. Beat eggs with pepper in a bowl and pour them into the skillet.
4. Stir cook for 5 minutes, then remove it from the heat.
5. Add bacon and mix well.
6. Divide the dough into 5 biscuits and slice each into 2 layers.
7. Press each biscuit into a 4-inch round.
8. Add a tablespoon of the egg mixture at the center of each round and top it with a piece of cheese.
9. Carefully fold the biscuit dough around the filling and pinch the edges to seal.
10. Whisk egg with water in a small bowl and brush the egg wash over the biscuits.
11. Place the biscuit bombs in the Air Fryer Basket and spray them with cooking oil.
12. Place the Air Fryer Basket again in the Air Fryer and cook for 14 minutes.
13. Press the START/PAUSE BUTTON to begin cooking.
14. Flip the egg bombs when cooked halfway through, then resume cooking.
15. Serve warm.

Serving Suggestion: Serve the eggs balls with crispy bacon.

Variation Tip: Add dried herbs to the egg filling.

Nutrition:

CALORIES 102 | FAT 7.6G |SODIUM 545MG | CARBS 1.5G | FIBER 0.4G | SUGAR 0.7G | PROTEIN 7.1G

BREAKFAST SAUSAGE OMELET

 **PREPARATION TIME**
10 MINUTES

 COOKING TIME
15 MINUTES

 SERVINGS
2 PERSONS

INGREDIENTS:

- ¼ pound breakfast sausage, cooked and crumbled
- 4 eggs, beaten
- ½ cup pepper Jack cheese blend
- 2 tablespoons green bell pepper, sliced
- 1 green onion, chopped
- 1 pinch cayenne pepper
- Cooking spray

PREPARATIONS:

1. Take a bowl and whisk eggs in it along with crumbled sausage, pepper Jack cheese, green onions, red bell pepper, and cayenne pepper.
2. Mix it all well.
3. Take a cake pan that fits side the Ninja air fryer and grease it with oil spray.
4. Pour the omelet mixture into the cake pan.
5. Select AIR FRY mode for 3 minutes at 325 degrees F to preheat the air fryer
6. Press START/PAUSE to start the preheating process.
7. Once preheating is done, put the cake pan inside the basket and place the basket inside the unit.
8. Turn on the Air Fry function and let it cook for 15-20 minutes at 310 degrees F.
9. Once the cooking cycle completes, take out, and serve hot, as a delicious breakfast.

Serving Suggestion: Serve it with ketchup.
Variation Tip: Use Parmesan cheese instead of pepper jack Cheese

Nutrition:

CALORIES 691| FAT 52.4G | SODIUM 1122 MG | CARBS 13.3G | FIBER 1.8G| SUGAR 7G | PROTEIN 42G

BANANA AND RAISINS MUFFINS

 PREPARATION TIME
20 MINUTES

 COOKING TIME
16 MINUTES

 SERVINGS
2 PERSONS

INGREDIENTS:

- Salt, pinch
- 2 eggs, whisked
- ⊠ cup butter, melted
- 4 tablespoons almond milk
- ¼ teaspoon vanilla extract
- ½ teaspoon baking powder
- 1 ½ cups all-purpose flour
- 1 cup mashed bananas
- 2 tablespoons raisins

PREPARATIONS:

1. Select AIR FRY mode for 3 minutes at 325 degrees F to preheat the air fryer
2. Press START/PAUSE to start the preheating process.
3. Once preheating is done, press START/PAUSE.
4. Take about 4 large (one-cup sized) ramekins and layer them with muffin papers.
5. Crack eggs in a large bowl, and Combine well and start adding vanilla extract, almond milk, baking powder, and melted butter.
6. Whisk the ingredients very well.
7. Take a separate bowl and add the all-purpose flour, and salt.
8. Now, combine the add dry ingredients with the wet ingredients.
9. Now, pour mashed bananas and raisins into this batter.
10. Mix it well to make a batter for the muffins.
11. Now pour the batter into 4 ramekins and place the ramekins in the air fryer basket.
12. Set the timer to 16 minutes at 350 degrees F at AIR FRY mode.
13. Check if not done, and let it AIR FRY for one more minute.
14. Once it is done, serve.

Serving Suggestion: None
Variation Tip: None

Nutrition:

CALORIES 727| FAT 43.1G| SODIUM366 MG | CARBS 74.4G | FIBER 4.7G | SUGAR 16.1G | PROTEIN 14.1G

EGG WITH BABY SPINACH

 **PREPARATION TIME**
12 MINUTES

 **COOKING TIME**
12 MINUTES

 SERVINGS
4 PERSONS

INGREDIENTS:

- Nonstick spray, for greasing ramekins
- 2 tablespoons olive oil
- 6 ounces baby spinach
- 2 garlic cloves, minced
- ⊠ teaspoon kosher salt
- 6-8 large eggs
- ½ cup half and half
- Salt and black pepper, to taste
- 8 Sourdough bread slices, toasted

PREPARATIONS:

1. Preheat the unit by selecting AIR FRY mode for 2 minutes at 350 degrees F.
2. Press START/PAUSE to start the preheating process.
3. Once preheating is done, press START/PAUSE.
4. Grease 4 ramekins with oil spray and set aside for further use.
5. Take a skillet and heat oil in it.
6. Then cook spinach for 2 minutes and add garlic and salt black pepper.
7. Let it simmer for 2 more minutes.
8. Once the spinach is wilted, transfer it to a plate.
9. Whisk an egg into a small bowl.
10. Add in the spinach.
11. Whisk it well and then pour half and half.
12. Divide this mixture between 4 ramekins and remember not to overfill it to the top, leave a little space on top.
13. Put the ramekins in the basket of the Ninja Foodi Air Fryer.
14. Select AIR FRY mode at 350 degrees F for 12 minutes. Press START/PAUSE to initiate cooking.
15. Once it's cooked and eggs are done, serve with sourdough bread slices.

Serving Suggestion: Serve it with cream cheese topping.

Variation Tip: Use plain bread slices instead of sourdough bread slices.

Nutrition:

CALORIES 404| FAT 19.6G| SODIUM 761MG | CARBS 40.1G | FIBER 2.5G | SUGAR 2.5G | PROTEIN 19.2G

YELLOW POTATOES WITH EGGS

 PREPARATION TIME
10 MINUTES

 COOKING TIME
30 MINUTES

 SERVINGS
2 PERSONS

INGREDIENTS:

- 1 pound Dutch yellow potatoes, quartered
- 1 red bell pepper, chopped
- Salt and black pepper, to taste
- 1 green bell pepper, chopped
- 2 teaspoons olive oil
- 2 teaspoons garlic powder
- 1 teaspoon onion powder
- 1 egg
- ¼ teaspoon butter

PREPARATIONS:

1. Preheat the unit by selecting AIR FRY mode for 5 minutes at 325 degrees F.
2. Press START/PAUSE to start the preheating process.
3. Toss together diced potatoes, green pepper, red pepper, salt, black pepper, and olive oil along with garlic powder and onion powder.
4. Take ramekin and grease it with oil spray.
5. Whisk egg in a bowl and add salt and pepper along with ½ teaspoon of butter.
6. Pour egg into a ramekin and place ramekins inside the air fryer.
7. Transfer bowl ingredients to the air fryer basket aside from the ramekins.
8. Set the time for the basket to 30 minutes at 400 degrees F, on the AIR FRY mode.
9. Once preheating is done, press START/PAUSE.
10. Once 10 minutes pass, press PAUSE and take out the ramekin.
11. Press the START/PAUSE button, and let the potatoes cook for the remaining minutes.
12. Once done, serve and enjoy.

Serving Suggestion: Serve it with sourdough toasted bread slices.

Variation Tip: Use white potatoes instead of yellow Dutch potatoes.

Nutrition:

CALORIES252 | FAT 7.5G | SODIUM 37MG | CARBS 40G | FIBER3.9G | SUGAR 7G | PROTEIN 6.7G

SNACKS & APPETIZERS

ONION RINGS

 **PREPARATION TIME**
10 MINUTES

 **COOKING TIME**
22 MINUTES

 SERVINGS
4 PERSONS

INGREDIENTS:

- ¾ cup all-purpose flour
- 1 teaspoon salt
- 1 large onion, cut into rings
- ½ cup cornstarch
- 2 teaspoons baking powder
- 1 cup low-fat milk
- 1 egg
- 1 cup bread crumbs
- ⅛ teaspoons paprika
- Cooking spray
- ⅛ teaspoons garlic powder

PREPARATIONS:

1. Preheat your Air Fryer to 390°F using Air Fry mode.
2. Mix flour with baking powder, cornstarch, and salt in a small bowl.
3. First, coat the onion rings with flour mixture; set them aside.
4. Beat milk with egg, then add the remaining flour mixture into the egg.
5. Mix them well together to make a thick batter.
6. Now dip the floured onion rings into the prepared batter and coat them well.
7. Place the rings on a wire rack for 10 minutes.
8. Spread bread crumbs in a shallow bowl.
9. Coat the onion rings with breadcrumbs and shake off the excess.
10. Set the coated onion rings in the Air Fryer Basket.
11. Spray all the rings with the cooking spray.
12. Place the Air Fryer Basket again in the Air Fryer and cook for 22 minutes.
13. Press the START/PAUSE BUTTON to begin cooking.
14. Flip once cooked halfway through, then resume cooking 15. Season the air-fried onion rings with garlic powder and paprika.
15. Serve.

Serving Suggestion: Serve with tomato sauce or cream cheese dip.

Variation Tip: Use crushed cornflakes for breading to have extra crispiness.

Nutrition:

CALORIES 229 | FAT 1.9 |SODIUM 567MG | CARBS 1.9G | FIBER 0.4G | SUGAR 0.6G | PROTEIN 11.8G

CRISPY TORTILLA CHIPS

 **PREPARATION TIME**
15 MINUTES

 **COOKING TIME**
13 MINUTES

 SERVINGS
8 PERSONS

INGREDIENTS:

- 4 (6-inch) corn tortillas
- 1 tablespoon avocado oil
- Sea salt to taste
- Cooking spray

PREPARATIONS:

1. Preheat your Air Fryer to 390°F using Air Fry mode.
2. Spread the corn tortillas on the working surface.
3. Slice them into bite-sized triangles.
4. Toss them with salt and cooking oil.
5. Place the triangles in the Air Fryer Basket in a single layer.
6. Place the Air Fryer Basket again in the Air Fryer and cook for 13 minutes.
7. Press the START/PAUSE BUTTON to begin cooking.
8. Toss the chips once cooked halfway through, then resume cooking.
9. Serve and enjoy.

Serving Suggestion: Serve with guacamole, mayonnaise, or cream cheese dip.

Variation Tip: Drizzle parmesan cheese on top before air frying.

Nutrition:

CALORIES 103 | FAT 8.4G |SODIUM 117MG | CARBS 3.5G | FIBER 0.9G | SUGAR 1.5G | PROTEIN 5.1G

PARMESAN FRENCH FRIES

 **PREPARATION TIME**
10 MINUTES

 **COOKING TIME**
20 MINUTES

 SERVINGS
6 PERSONS

INGREDIENTS:

- 3 medium russet potatoes
- 2 tablespoons parmesan cheese
- 2 tablespoons fresh parsley, chopped
- 1 tablespoon olive oil
- Salt, to taste

PREPARATIONS:

1. Preheat your Air Fryer to 390°F using Air Fry mode.
2. Wash the potatoes and pass them through the fries' cutter to get ¼-inch-thick fries.
3. Place the fries in a colander and drizzle salt on top.
4. Leave these fries for 10 minutes, then rinse.
5. Toss the potatoes with parmesan cheese, oil, salt, and parsley in a bowl.
6. Place the potatoes into the Air Fryer Basket.
7. Place the Air Fryer Basket again in the Air Fryer and cook for 20 minutes.
8. Press the START/PAUSE BUTTON to begin cooking.
9. Toss the chips once cooked halfway through, then resume cooking.
10. Serve warm.

Serving Suggestion: Serve with tomato ketchup, Asian coleslaw, or creamed cabbage.

Variation Tip: Toss fries with black pepper for a change in taste.

Nutrition:

CALORIES 307 | FAT 8.6G | SODIUM 510MG | CARBS 22.2G | FIBER 1.4G | SUGAR 13G | PROTEIN 33.6G

FRIED HALLOUMI CHEESE

 **PREPARATION TIME**
10 MINUTES

 **COOKING TIME**
12 MINUTES

 SERVINGS
6 PERSONS

INGREDIENTS:

- 1 block halloumi cheese, sliced
- 2 teaspoons olive oil

PREPARATIONS:

1. Preheat your Air Fryer to 390°F using Air Fry mode.
2. Place the halloumi cheese slices in the Air Fryer Basket.
3. Drizzle olive oil over the cheese slices.
4. Place the Air Fryer Basket again in the Air Fryer and cook for 12 minutes.
5. Flip the cheese slices once cooked halfway through.
6. Serve.

Serving Suggestion: Serve with fresh yogurt dip or cucumber salad.

Variation Tip: Add black pepper and salt for seasoning.

Nutrition:

CALORIES 186 | FAT 3G |SODIUM 223MG | CARBS 31G | FIBER 8.7G |

SWEET BITES

 **PREPARATION TIME**
25 MINUTES

 **COOKING TIME**
10 MINUTES

 SERVINGS
4 PERSONS

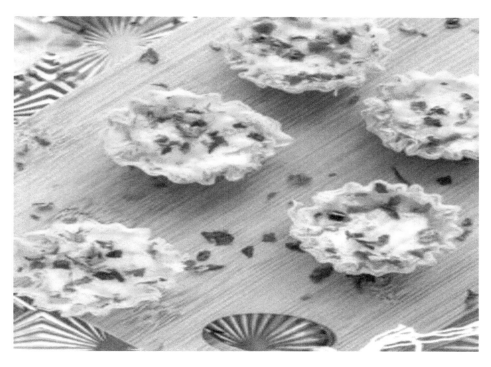

INGREDIENTS:

- 10 sheets of Phyllo dough, (filo dough)
- 2 tablespoons melted butter
- 1 cup walnuts, chopped
- 2 teaspoons honey
- 1 Pinch cinnamon
- 1 teaspoon orange zest

PREPARATIONS:

1. Preheat the unit by selecting AIR FRY mode for 2 minutes at 325 degrees F.
2. Press START/PAUSE to start the preheating process.
3. Once preheating is done, press START/PAUSE.
4. First, layer together 10 Phyllo dough sheets on a flat surface.
5. Then cut it into 4*4-inch squares.
6. Now, coat the squares with butter, drizzle some honey, orange zest, walnuts, and cinnamon.
7. Bring all 4 corners together and press the corners to make a little purse-like design.
8. Put it inside the air fryer basket and select the AIR FRY mode and set it for 10 minutes at 375 degrees F.
9. Once done, take out and serve.

Serving Suggestion: Serve with a topping of nuts.

Variation Tip: None.

Nutrition:

CALORIES 397 | FAT 27.1 G | SODIUM 271MG | CARBS31.2 G | FIBER 3.2G | SUGAR3.3G | PROTEIN 11G

PEPPERED ASPARAGUS

PREPARATION TIME
10 MINUTES

COOKING TIME
16 MINUTES

SERVINGS
6 PERSONS

INGREDIENTS:

- 1 bunch of asparagus, trimmed
- Avocado or olive oil
- Himalayan salt, to taste
- Black pepper, to taste

PREPARATIONS:

1. Preheat your Air Fryer to 390°F using Air Fry mode.
2. Place the asparagus in the Air Fryer Basket.
3. Toss the asparagus with salt, black pepper, and oil.
4. Place the Air Fryer Basket again in the Air Fryer and cook for 16 minutes.
5. Press the START/PAUSE BUTTON to begin cooking.
6. Serve warm.

Serving Suggestion: Serve with mayonnaise or cream cheese dip.

Variation Tip: Use panko crumbs for breading to have extra crispiness.

Nutrition:

CALORIES 163 | FAT 11.5G |SODIUM 918MG | CARBS 8.3G | FIBER 4.2G | SUGAR 0.2G | PROTEIN 7.4G

CHEDDAR QUICHE

 **PREPARATION TIME**
10 MINUTES

 **COOKING TIME**
12 MINUTES

 SERVINGS
2 PERSONS

INGREDIENTS:

- 4 eggs, organic
- 1 ¼ cups heavy cream
- Salt, pinch
- ½ cup broccoli florets
- ½ cup cheddar cheese, shredded and for sprinkling

PREPARATIONS:

1. Take a Pyrex pitcher and crack two eggs in it.
2. And fill it with heavy cream, about half the way up.
3. Add in the salt and then add in the broccoli and pour this into a quiche dish, and top it with shredded cheddar cheese.
4. Preheat the unit by selecting AIR FRY mode for 2 minutes at 325 degrees F.
5. Press START/PAUSE to start the preheating process.
6. Once preheating is done, press START/PAUSE.
7. Now put the dish inside the air fryer basket.
8. Set the time to 12 minutes at 325 degrees F.
9. Once done, serve hot.

Serving Suggestion: Serve with herbs as a topping.

Variation Tip: Use spinach instead of broccoli florets.

Nutrition:

CALORIES 454 | FAT 40G | SODIUM 406MG | CARBS 4.2G | FIBER 0.6G| SUGAR1.3 G | PROTEIN 20G

CRISPY PLANTAIN CHIPS

 **PREPARATION TIME**
15 MINUTES

 **COOKING TIME**
20 MINUTES

 SERVINGS
4 PERSONS

INGREDIENTS:

- 1 green plantain
- 1 teaspoon canola oil
- ½ teaspoons sea salt

PREPARATIONS:

1. At 350 degrees F, preheat your Air Fryer on Air Fry mode.
2. Peel and cut the plantains into long strips using a mandolin slicer.
3. Grease the Air Fryer Basket with a ½ teaspoon of canola oil.
4. Toss the plantains with salt and remaining canola oil.
5. Place these plantains in the Air Fryer Basket.
6. Place the Air Fryer Basket again in the Air Fryer and cook for 20 minutes.
7. Toss the plantains after 10 minutes and resume cooking.
8. Serve warm.

Serving Suggestion: Serve with cream cheese dip and celery sticks.

Variation Tip: Use black pepper to season the chips.

Nutrition:

CALORIES 122 | FAT 1.8G |SODIUM 794MG | CARBS 17G | FIBER 8.9G | SUGAR 1.6G | PROTEIN 14.9G

GRILL CHEESE SANDWICH

 **PREPARATION TIME** 15 MINUTES

 **COOKING TIME** 10 MINUTES

 SERVINGS 2 PERSONS

INGREDIENTS:

- 4 slices white bread slices
- 2 tablespoons of butter, melted
- 2 slices sharp cheddar
- 2 slices Swiss cheese
- 2 slices mozzarella cheese

PREPARATIONS:

1. Preheat the unit by selecting AIR FRY mode for 2 minutes at 325 degrees F.
2. Press START/PAUSE to start the preheating process.
3. Once preheating is done, press START/PAUSE.
4. Brush melted butter on one side of all the bread slices and then top the 2
5. bread slices with slices of cheddar, Swiss, and mozzarella, one slice per bread.
6. Top it with the other slice to make a sandwich.
7. Add it to the basket of the air fryer.
8. Turn on AIR FRY mode at 350 degrees F for 10 minutes.
9. Once done, serve.

Serving Suggestion: Serve with tomato soup.
Variation Tip: Use oil spray instead of butter.

Nutrition:

CALORIES 577 | FAT 38G | SODIUM 1466MG | CARBS 30.5G | FIBER 1.1G| SUGAR 6.5G | PROTEIN 27.6G

CHICKEN CRESCENT WRAPS

 PREPARATION TIME
10 MINUTES

 COOKING TIME
12 MINUTES

 SERVINGS
6 PERSONS

INGREDIENTS:

- 3 tablespoons chopped onion
- 3 garlic cloves, peeled and minced
- ¾ (8 ounces) package cream cheese
- 6 tablespoons butter
- 2 boneless chicken breasts, cubed, cooked
- 3 (10 ounces) cans of refrigerated crescent roll dough

PREPARATIONS:

1. Preheat your Air Fryer to 390°F using Air Fry mode.
2. Heat oil in a skillet and add onion and garlic to sauté until soft.
3. Add cooked chicken, sautéed veggies, butter, and cream cheese to a blender.
4. Blend well until smooth. Spread the crescent dough over a flat surface.
5. Slice the dough into 12 rectangles.
6. Spoon the chicken mixture at the center of each rectangle.
7. Roll the dough to wrap the mixture and form a ball.
8. Place these balls in the Air Fryer Basket.
9. Place the Air Fryer Basket again in the Air Fryer and cook for 12 minutes.
10. Press the START/PAUSE BUTTON to begin cooking.
11. Serve warm.

Serving Suggestion: Serve with tomato sauce or cream cheese dip.

Variation Tip: You can also prepare the filling using leftover turkey or pork.

Nutrition:

CALORIES 100 | FAT 2G |SODIUM 480MG | CARBS 4G | FIBER 2G | SUGAR 0G | PROTEIN 18G

BLUEBERRIES MUFFINS

 **PREPARATION TIME**
15 MINUTES

 **COOKING TIME**
15 MINUTES

 SERVINGS
2 PERSONS

INGREDIENTS:

- Salt, pinch
- 2 eggs
- ⅓ cup sugar
- ⅓ cup vegetable oil
- 4 tablespoons water
- 1 teaspoon lemon zest
- ¼ teaspoon vanilla extract
- ½ teaspoon baking powder
- 1 cup all-purpose flour
- 1 cup blueberries

PREPARATIONS:

1. Take 4 one-cup-sized ramekins that are oven safe and layer them with muffin papers.
2. Take a bowl and whisk the egg, sugar, oil, water, vanilla extract, and lemon zest.
3. Whisk it all very well.
4. Now, in a separate bowl, mix the flour, baking powder, and salt.
5. Now, add dry ingredients slowly to wet ingredients.
6. Now, pour this batter into ramekins and top it with blueberries.
7. Preheat the unit by selecting AIR FRY mode for 2 minutes at 325 degrees F.
8. Press START/PAUSE to start the preheating process.
9. Once preheating is done, press START/PAUSE.
10. Now, place the ramekins inside the Ninja Foodi Air Fryer.
11. Set the time to AIR FRY mode for 15 minutes at 350 degrees F.
12. Check if not done, and let it AIR FRY for one more minute.
13. Once it is done, serve.

Serving Suggestion: Serve it with whipped cream topping.

Variation Tip: Use butter instead of vegetable oil.

Nutrition:

CALORIES 781 | FAT 41.6G | SODIUM 143MG | CARBS 92.7G | FIBER 3.5G | SUGAR41.2 G | PROTEIN 0G

CHICKEN TENDERS

 **PREPARATION TIME**
15 MINUTES

 **COOKING TIME**
12 MINUTES

 SERVINGS
3 PERSONS

INGREDIENTS:

- 1-pound chicken tender
- Salt and black pepper, to taste
- 1 cup Panko bread crumbs
- 2 cups Italian bread crumbs
- 1 cup parmesan cheese
- 2 eggs
- Oil spray, for greasing

PREPARATIONS:

1. Sprinkle the tenders with salt and black pepper.
2. In a medium bowl, mix Panko bread crumbs with Italian breadcrumbs.
3. Add salt, pepper, and parmesan cheese.
4. Crack two eggs in a bowl.
5. First, put the chicken tender in eggs.
6. Now dredge the tender in a bowl and coat the tender well with crumbs.
7. Preheat the unit by selecting AIR FRY mode for 2 minutes at 325 degrees F.
8. Press START/PAUSE to start the preheating process.
9. Once preheating is done, press START/PAUSE.
10. Line the basket of the air fryer with parchment paper.
11. At the end, spray the tenders with oil spray.
12. Layer the tenders inside the basket of Ninja Foodi Air Fryer.
13. Set it to the AIR FRY mode at 350 degrees F for 12 minutes.
14. Once it's done, serve.

Serving Suggestion: Serve it with ranch or ketchup.

Variation Tip: Use Italian seasoning instead of Italian bread crumbs.

Nutrition:

CALORIES558 | FAT23.8G | SODIUM872 MG | CARBS 20.9G | FIBER1.7 G| SUGAR2.2G | PROTEIN 63.5G

FISH & SEAFOOD

SALMON PATTIES

 **PREPARATION TIME**
15 MINUTES

 **COOKING TIME**
18 MINUTES

 **SERVINGS**
8 PERSONS

Ingredients:

- 1 lb. fresh Atlantic salmon side
- ¼ cup avocado, mashed
- ¼ cup cilantro, diced
- 1 ½ teaspoon yellow curry powder
- ½ teaspoons sea salt
- ¼ cup, 4 teaspoons tapioca starch
- 2 brown eggs
- ½ cup coconut flakes
- Coconut oil, melted, for brushing
- For the greens:
- 2 teaspoons organic coconut oil, melted
- 6 cups arugula & spinach mix, tightly packed Pinch of sea salt

Preparations:

1. Preheat your Air Fryer to 390ºF using Air Fry mode.
2. Remove the fish skin and dice the flesh.
3. Place in a large bowl. Add cilantro, avocado, salt, and curry powder mix gently.
4. Add tapioca starch and mix well again.
5. Make 8 salmon patties out of this mixture, about a half-inch thick.
6. Place them on a baking sheet lined with wax paper and freeze them for 20 minutes.
7. Place ¼ cup of tapioca starch and coconut flakes on a flat plate.
8. Dip the patties in the whisked egg, then coat the frozen patties in the starch and flakes.
9. Place the patties in the Air Fryer Basket and spray them with cooking oil.
10. Place the Air Fryer Basket again in the Air Fryer and cook for 17 minutes.
11. Press the START/PAUSE BUTTON to begin cooking.
12. Flip the patties once cooked halfway through, then resume cooking.
13. Sauté arugula with spinach in coconut oil in a pan for 30 seconds.
14. Serve the patties with sautéed greens mixture.

Serving Suggestion: Serve with sautéed green beans or asparagus.

Variation Tip: Add lemon juice to the mixture before mixing.

Nutrition:

CALORIES 260 | FAT 16G |SODIUM 585MG | CARBS 3.1G | FIBER 1.3G | SUGAR 0.2G | PROTEIN 25.5G

SALMON NUGGETS

PREPARATION TIME
15 MINUTES

COOKING TIME
15 MINUTES

SERVINGS
4 PERSONS

Ingredients:

- ⅓ cup maple syrup
- ¼ teaspoon dried chipotle pepper
- 1 pinch sea salt
- 1 ½ cups croutons
- 1 large egg
- 1 (1 pound) skinless salmon fillet, cut into 1 ½-inch chunk
- Cooking spray

Preparations:

1. Preheat your Air Fryer to 390°F using Air Fry mode.
2. Mix chipotle powder, maple syrup, and salt in a saucepan and cook on a simmer for 5 minutes.
3. Crush the croutons in a food processor and transfer them to a bowl.
4. Beat egg in another shallow bowl.
5. Season the salmon chunks with sea salt.
6. Dip the salmon in the egg, then coat with breadcrumbs.
7. Spread the coated salmon chunks in the Air Fryer Basket.
8. Place the Air Fryer Basket again in the Air Fryer and cook for 10 minutes.
9. Press the START/PAUSE BUTTON to begin cooking.
10. Flip the chunks once cooked halfway through, then resume cooking.
11. Pour the maple syrup on top and serve warm.

Serving Suggestion: Serve with creamy dip and crispy fries.

Variation Tip: Use crushed cornflakes for breading to have extra crispiness.

Nutrition:

CALORIES 275 | FAT 1.4G |SODIUM 582MG | CARBS 31.5G | FIBER 1.1G | SUGAR 0.1G | PROTEIN 29.8G

BREADED SCALLOPS

 **PREPARATION TIME**
15 MINUTES

 **COOKING TIME**
12 MINUTES

 **SERVINGS**
4 PERSONS

Ingredients:

- ½ cup crushed buttery crackers
- ½ teaspoon garlic powder
- ½ teaspoon seafood seasoning
- 2 tablespoons butter, melted
- 1-pound sea scallops patted dry
- Cooking spray

Preparations:

1. Preheat your Air Fryer to 390°F using Air Fry mode.
2. Mix cracker crumbs, garlic powder, and seafood seasoning in a shallow bowl. Spread melted butter in another shallow bowl.
3. Dip each scallop in the melted butter and then roll in the breading to coat well.
4. Grease the Air Fryer Basket with cooking spray and place the scallops inside.
5. Place the Air Fryer Basket again in the Air Fryer and cook for 12 minutes.
6. Press the START/PAUSE BUTTON to begin cooking.
7. Flip the scallops with a spatula after 4 minutes and resume cooking.
8. Serve warm.

Serving Suggestion: Serve with creamy dip and crispy fries.

Variation Tip: Use crushed cornflakes for breading to have extra crispiness.

Nutrition:

CALORIES 275 | FAT 1.4G |SODIUM 582MG | CARBS 31.5G | FIBER 1.1G | SUGAR 0.1G | PROTEIN 29.8G

FRIED LOBSTER TAILS

 **PREPARATION TIME**
10 MINUTES

 **COOKING TIME**
18 MINUTES

 **SERVINGS**
4 PERSONS

Ingredients:

- 4 (4 oz.) lobster tails
- 8 tablespoons butter, melted
- 2 teaspoons lemon zest
- 2 garlic cloves, grated
- Salt and black pepper ground to taste
- 2 teaspoons fresh parsley, chopped
- 4 wedges lemon

Preparations:

1. At 350 degrees F, preheat your Air Fryer on Air Fry mode.
2. Spread the lobster tails into butterflies, slit the top to expose the lobster meat while keeping the tail intact.
3. Place the lobster tails in the Air Fryer Basket with their lobster meat facing up.
4. Mix melted butter with lemon zest and garlic in a bowl.
5. Brush the butter mixture on top of the lobster tails.
6. And drizzle salt and black pepper on top.
7. Place the Air Fryer Basket again in the Air Fryer and cook for 18 minutes.
8. Press the START/PAUSE BUTTON to begin cooking.
9. Garnish with parsley and lemon wedges.
10. Serve warm.

Serving Suggestion: Serve on a bed of lettuce leaves.

Variation Tip: Drizzle crushed cornflakes on top to have extra crispiness.

Nutrition:

CALORIES 257 | FAT 10.4G |SODIUM 431MG | CARBS 20G | FIBER 0G | SUGAR 1.6G | PROTEIN 21G

SCALLOPS WITH GREENS

PREPARATION TIME
15 MINUTES

COOKING TIME
13 MINUTES

SERVINGS
8 PERSONS

Ingredients:

- ¾ cup heavy whipping cream
- 1 tablespoon tomato paste
- 1 tablespoon chopped fresh basil
- 1 teaspoon garlic, minced
- ½ teaspoon salt
- ½ teaspoon pepper
- 12 ounces frozen spinach thawed
- 8 jumbo sea scallops
- Vegetable oil to spray

Preparations:

1. Preheat your Air Fryer to 390°F using Air Fry mode.
2. Season the scallops with vegetable oil, salt, and pepper in a bowl.
3. Mix cream with spinach, basil, garlic, salt, pepper, and tomato paste in a bowl.
4. Pour this mixture over the scallops and mix gently.
5. Place the scallops in the Air Fryers Basket without using the crisper plate.
6. Place the Air Fryer Basket again in the Air Fryer and cook for 13 minutes.
7. Press the START/PAUSE BUTTON to begin cooking.
8. Serve right away.

Serving Suggestion: Serve with fresh cucumber salad.

Variation Tip: Use crushed cornflakes for breading to have extra crispiness.

Nutrition:

CALORIES 266 | FAT 6.3G |SODIUM 193MG | CARBS 39.1G | FIBER 7.2G | SUGAR 5.2G | PROTEIN 14.8G

TWO-WAY SALMON

 **PREPARATION TIME**
10 MINUTES

 **COOKING TIME**
18 MINUTES

 **SERVINGS**
2 PERSONS

Ingredients:

- 2 salmon fillets, 8 ounces each
- 2 tablespoons Cajun seasoning
- 2 tablespoons jerk seasoning
- 1 lemon cut in half
- Oil spray, for greasing

Preparations:

1. First, drizzle lemon juice over the salmon and wash it with tap water.
2. Rinse and pat dry the fillets with a paper towel.
3. Now rub o fillet with Cajun seasoning and grease it with oil spray.
4. Take the second fillet and rub it with jerk seasoning.
5. Grease the second fillet of salmon with oil spray.
6. Now put the salmon fillets in the air fryer basket.
7. Set the basket to 390 degrees F for 16-18 minutes at AIR FRY mode.
8. Hit the START/PAUSE button to start cooking.
9. Once the cooking is done, serve the fish fillets hot with mayonnaise.

Serving Suggestion: Serve it with ranch.
Variation Tip: None.

Nutrition:

CALORIES 238| FAT 11.8G| SODIUM 488MG | CARBS 9G | FIBER 0G | SUGAR 8G | PROTEIN 35G

SEAFOOD SHRIMP OMELET

 **PREPARATION TIME**
20 MINUTES

 **COOKING TIME**
15 MINUTES

 SERVINGS
2 PERSONS

Ingredients:

- 6 large shrimp, shells removed and chopped
- 6 eggs, beaten
- ½ tablespoon butter, melted
- 2 tablespoons green onions, sliced
- ⅓ cup mushrooms, chopped
- 1 pinch paprika
- Salt and black pepper, to taste
- Oil spray, for greasing

Preparations:

1. In a large bowl, whisk the eggs and add chopped shrimp, butter, green onions, mushrooms, paprika, salt, and black pepper.
2. Take a cake pan that fits inside the air fryer and grease them with oil spray.
3. Pour the egg mixture into the cake pan and place it inside the basket of the air fryer.
4. Turn on the Air Fry function, and let it cook for 15 minutes at 320
5. degrees F.
6. Once the cooking cycle completes, take out, and serve hot.

Serving Suggestion: Serve it with rice.
Variation Tip: Use olive oil for greasing purposes.

Nutrition:

CALORIES 300 | FAT 17.5G| SODIUM 368MG | CARBS 2.9G | FIBER 0.3G | SUGAR1.4G | PROTEIN32.2 G

SALMON WITH GREEN BEANS

 **PREPARATION TIME**
12 MINUTES

 COOKING TIME
18 MINUTES

 SERVINGS
1 PERSONS

Ingredients:

- 1 salmon fillet, 2 inches thick
- 2 teaspoons olive oil
- 2 teaspoons smoked paprika
- Salt and black pepper, to taste
- 1 cup green beans
- Oil spray, for greasing

Preparations:

1. Grease the green beans with oil spray and set them aside for further use,
2. Now rub the salmon fillet with olive oil, smoked paprika, salt, and black pepper.
3. Put the salmon fillets in the basket of the air fryer along with green beans.
4. You can adjust the green beans on a rack as well.
5. Now set it to AIR FRY mode at 350 degrees F for 18 minutes.
6. Once done, take out the salmon and green beans and transfer them to the serving plates and enjoy.

Serving Suggestion: Serve it with ranch dressing.
Variation Tip: Use any other green vegetable of your choice.

Nutrition:

CALORIES 367| FAT 22G| SODIUM 87MG | CARBS 10.2G | FIBER 5.3G | SUGAR 2G | PROTEIN 37.2G

FISH AND CHIPS

 **PREPARATION TIME**
15 MINUTES

 **COOKING TIME**
22 MINUTES

 **SERVINGS**
2 PERSONS

Ingredients:

- 1 pound potatoes, cut lengthwise
- 1 cup seasoned flour
- 2 eggs, organic
- ⅓ cup buttermilk
- 2 cup seafood fry mix
- ½ cup bread crumbs
- 2 codfish fillets, 6 ounces each
- Oil spray, for greasing

Preparations:

1. Take a bowl and whisk eggs in it along with buttermilk.
2. In a separate bowl, mix seafood fry mix and bread crumbs
3. Take a baking tray and spread flour on it.
4. Dip the fillets first in egg wash, then in flour, and at the end coat it with breadcrumbs mixture.
5. Put the fish fillet in the air fryer basket.
6. Grease the fish fillet with oil spray.
7. Put potato chips inside the basket and lightly grease them with oil spray.
8. Set the air fryer to AIR FRY mode at 400 degrees F for 22 minutes.
9. After 12 minutes take out the fish and continue with the cooking cycle.
10. Once done, serve and enjoy.

Serving Suggestion: Serve it with mayonnaise.
Variation Tip: Use water instead of buttermilk.

Nutrition:

CALORIES 992| FAT 22.3G| SODIUM1406 MG | CARBS 153.6G | FIBER 10G | SUGAR 10G | PROTEIN 40G

FROZEN BREADED FISH FILLET

 PREPARATION TIME 15 MINUTES

 COOKING TIME 12 MINUTES

 SERVINGS 2 PERSONS

Ingredients:

- 4 frozen breaded fish fillet
- Oil spray, for greasing
- 1 cup mayonnaise

Preparations:

1. Take the frozen fish fillets out of the bag and place them in the basket of the air fryer.
2. Lightly grease it with oil spray.
3. Set the unit to 380 degrees F for 12 minutes at AIR FRY mode.
4. Hit the START/PAUSE button to start cooking.
5. Once the cooking is done, serve the fish hot with mayonnaise.

Serving Suggestion: Serve it with salad and rice.
Variation Tip: Use olive oil instead of butter.

Nutrition:

CALORIES 921| FAT 61.5G| SODIUM 1575MG | CARBS 69G | FIBER 2G | SUGAR 9.5G | PROTEIN 29.1G

KETO BAKED SALMON WITH PESTO

 PREPARATION TIME
15 MINUTES

 COOKING TIME
18 MINUTES

 SERVINGS
2 PERSONS

Ingredients:

- 4 salmon fillets, 2 inches thick
- 2 ounces green pesto
- Salt and black pepper
- ½ tablespoon canola oil, for greasing

Ingredients for Green Sauce

- 1-½ cup mayonnaise
- 2 tablespoons Greek yogurt
- Salt and black pepper, to taste

Preparations:

1. Rub the salmon with pesto, salt, oil, and black pepper.
2. In a small bowl, whisk together all the green sauce ingredients.
3. Put the fish fillets in the basket.
4. Set the AIR FRY mode for 18 minutes at 390 degrees F.
5. Once the cooking is done, serve it with green sauce drizzle.
6. Enjoy.

Serving Suggestion: Serve it with mashed cheesy potatoes.

Variation Tip: Use butter instead of canal oil.

Nutrition:

CALORIES 1165 | FAT80.7 G| SODIUM 1087 MG | CARBS 33.1G | FIBER 0.5G | SUGAR11.5 G | PROTEIN 80.6G

CRUSTED TILAPIA

 **PREPARATION TIME**
20 MINUTES

 **COOKING TIME**
17 MINUTES

 **SERVINGS**
4 PERSONS

Ingredients:

- ¾ cup breadcrumbs
- 1 packet dry ranch-style dressing
- 2 ½ tablespoons vegetable oil
- 2 eggs beaten
- 4 tilapia fillets
- Herbs and chilies to garnish

Preparations:

1. Preheat your Air Fryer to 390°F using Air Fry mode.
2. Thoroughly mix ranch dressing with panko in a bowl.
3. Whisk eggs in a shallow bowl.
4. Dip each fish fillet in the egg, then coat evenly with the panko mixture.
5. Set two coated fillets in the Air Fryer Basket.
6. Place the Air Fryer Basket again in the Air Fryer and cook for 17 minutes.
7. Press the START/PAUSE BUTTON to begin cooking.
8. Serve warm with herbs and chilies

Serving Suggestion: Serve with sautéed asparagus on the side.

Variation Tip: Coat the fish with crushed cornflakes for extra crispiness.

Nutrition:

CALORIES 196 | FAT 7.1G |SODIUM 492MG | CARBS 21.6G | FIBER 2.9G | SUGAR 0.8G | PROTEIN 13.4G

CODFISH WITH HERB VINAIGRETTE

 **PREPARATION TIME**
15 MINUTES

 **COOKING TIME**
16 MINUTES

 SERVINGS
2 PERSONS

Ingredients:

- ½ cup parsley leaves
- 1 cup basil leaves
- ½ cup mint leaves
- 2 tablespoons thyme leaves
- ¼ teaspoon red pepper flakes
- 2 cloves garlic
- 4 tablespoons red wine vinegar
- ¼ cup olive oil
- Salt, to taste

Other Ingredients
- 1.5 pounds fish fillets, codfish
- 2 tablespoons olive oil
- Salt and black pepper, to taste
- 1 teaspoon paprika
- 1 teaspoon Italian seasoning

Preparations:

1. Blend the entire vinaigrette ingredient in a high-speed blender and pulse into a smooth paste.
2. Set aside for drizzling overcooked fish.
3. Rub the fillets with salt, black pepper, paprika, Italian seasoning, and olive oil.
4. Put it in the basket of the air fryer.
5. Set it to 16 minutes at 390 degrees F, on AIR FRY mode.
6. Once done, serve the fillets with the drizzle of blended vinaigrette.

Serving Suggestion: Serve it with rice.
Variation Tip: Use sour cream instead of cream cheese.

Nutrition:

CALORIES 1219| FAT 81.8G| SODIUM 1906MG | CARBS 64.4G | FIBER 5.5G | SUGAR 0.4G | PROTEIN 52.1G

LEMON PEPPER SALMON WITH ASPARAGUS

 **PREPARATION TIME**
20 MINUTES

 **COOKING TIME**
20 MINUTES

 **SERVINGS**
2 PERSONS

Ingredients:

- 1 cup green asparagus
- 2 tablespoons butter
- 2 fillets salmon, 8 ounces each
- Salt and black pepper, to taste
- 1 teaspoon lemon juice
- ½ teaspoon lemon zest
- Oil spray, for greasing

Preparations:

1. Rinse and trim the asparagus.
2. Rinse and pat dry the salmon fillets.
3. Take a bowl and mix lemon juice, lemon zest, salt, and black pepper.
4. Brush the fish fillet with the rub and place it in the basket along with asparagus.
5. Set it to AIR FRY mode for 20 minutes at 390 degrees F.
6. Once 5 minutes pass, take out the basket and remove asparagus.
7. Continue with the cooking cycle.
8. Once done, serve and enjoy.

Serving Suggestion: Serve it with baked potato.

Variation Tip: Use olive oil instead of butter.

Nutrition:

CALORIES 482| FAT 28G| SODIUM209 MG | CARBS 2.8G | FIBER1.5 G | SUGAR1.4 G | PROTEIN 56.3G

BEEF LAMB & PORK

BEEF CHEESEBURGERS

 **PREPARATION TIME**
15 MINUTES

 **COOKING TIME**
13 MINUTES

 **SERVINGS**
4 PERSONS

INGREDIENTS:

- 1 lb. ground beef
- Salt, to taste
- 2 garlic cloves, minced
- 1 tablespoon soy sauce
- Black pepper, to taste
- 4 American cheese slices
- 4 hamburger buns
- Mayonnaise, to serve
- Lettuce, to serve
- Sliced tomatoes, to serve
- Sliced red onion, to serve

PREPARATIONS:

1. Preheat your Air Fryer to 390°F using Air Fry mode.
2. Mix beef with soy sauce and garlic in a large bowl.
3. Make 4 patties, 4 inches in diameter.
4. Rub them with salt and black pepper on both sides.
5. Place the patties in the Air Fryer Basket.
6. Place the Air Fryer Basket again in the Air Fryer and cook for 13 minutes.
7. Press the START/PAUSE BUTTON to begin cooking.
8. Flip each patty once cooked halfway through, and resume cooking.
9. Add each patty to the hamburger buns along with mayo, tomatoes, onions, and lettuce.
10. Serve.

Serving Suggestion: Serve with tomato ketchup or chili sauce.

Variation Tip: Add breadcrumbs to the beef burger mixture for a crumbly texture.

Nutrition:

CALORIES 437 | FAT 28G |SODIUM 1221MG | CARBS 22.3G | FIBER 0.9G | SUGAR 8G | PROTEIN 30.3G

GOCHUJANG BRISKET

PREPARATION TIME
20 MINUTES

COOKING TIME
55 MINUTES

SERVINGS
6 PERSONS

INGREDIENTS:

- ½ tablespoon sweet paprika
- ½ teaspoon toasted sesame oil
- 2 lbs. beef brisket, cut into 4 pieces
- Salt, to taste
- ⅛ cup Gochujang, Korean chili paste
- Black pepper, to taste
- 1 small onion, diced
- 2 garlic cloves, minced
- 1 teaspoon Asian fish sauce
- 1 ½ tablespoons peanut oil, as needed
- ½ tablespoons fresh ginger, grated
- ¼ teaspoon red chili flakes
- ½ cup water
- 1 tablespoon ketchup
- 1 tablespoon soy sauce

PREPARATIONS:

1. Preheat your Air Fryer to 390°F using Air Fry mode.
2.
3. Thoroughly rub the beef brisket with olive oil, paprika, chili flakes, black pepper, and salt.
4. Place the brisket in the Air Fryer Basket.
5. Place the Air Fryer Basket again in the Air Fryer and cook for 35 minutes.
6. Press the START/PAUSE BUTTON to begin cooking.
7. Flip the brisket halfway through, and resume cooking.
8. Meanwhile, heat oil in a skillet and add ginger, onion, and garlic.
9. Sauté for 5 minutes, then add all the remaining ingredients.
10. Cook the mixture for 15 minutes approximately until well thoroughly mixed.
11. Serve the brisket with this sauce on top.

Serving Suggestion: Serve on top of boiled white rice.

Variation Tip: Add Worcestershire sauce and honey to taste.

Nutrition:

CALORIES 374 | FAT 25G |SODIUM 275MG | CARBS 7.3G | FIBER 0G | SUGAR 6G | PROTEIN 12.3G

CHIPOTLE BEEF

PREPARATION TIME
15 MINUTES

COOKING TIME
18 MINUTES

SERVINGS
4 PERSONS

INGREDIENTS:

- 1 lb. beef steak, cut into chunks
- 1 large egg
- ½ cup parmesan cheese, grated
- ½ cup pork panko
- ½ teaspoon seasoned salt

Chipotle Ranch Dip

- ¼ cup mayonnaise
- ¼ cup sour cream
- 1 teaspoon chipotle paste
- ½ teaspoon ranch dressing mix
- ¼ medium lime, juiced

PREPARATIONS:

1. Preheat your Air Fryer to 390°F using Air Fry mode.
2. Mix all the ingredients for chipotle ranch dip in a bowl.
3. Keep it in the refrigerator for 30 minutes.
4. Mix pork panko with salt and parmesan.
5. Beat egg in one bowl and spread the panko mixture in another flat bowl.
6. Dip the steak chunks in the egg first, then coat them with panko mixture.
7. Spread them in the Air Fryer Basket and spray them with cooking oil.
8. Place the Air Fryer Basket again in the Air Fryer and cook for 18 minutes.
9. Press the START/PAUSE BUTTON to begin cooking.
10. Serve with chipotle ranch and salt and pepper on top. Enjoy.

Serving Suggestion: Serve with tomato ketchup or chili sauce.

Variation Tip: Add crushed cornflakes for breading to get extra crisp.

Nutrition:

CALORIES 310 | FAT 17G |SODIUM 271MG | CARBS 4.3G | FIBER 0.9G | SUGAR 2.1G | PROTEIN 35G

MUSTARD RUBBED LAMB CHOPS

 PREPARATION TIME
15 MINUTES

 COOKING TIME
32 MINUTES

 SERVINGS
4 PERSONS

INGREDIENTS:

- 1 teaspoon Dijon mustard
- 1 teaspoon olive oil
- ½ teaspoon soy sauce
- ½ teaspoon garlic, minced
- ½ teaspoon cumin powder
- ½ teaspoon cayenne pepper
- ½ teaspoon Italian spice blend
- ⅛ teaspoon salt
- 4 pieces of lamb chops

PREPARATIONS:

1. At 350 degrees F, preheat your Air Fryer on Air Fry mode.
2. Mix Dijon mustard, soy sauce, olive oil, garlic, cumin powder, cayenne pepper, Italian spice blend, and salt in a medium bowl and mix well.
3. Place lamb chops into a Ziploc bag and pour in the marinade.
4. Press the air out of the bag and seal tightly.
5. Press the marinade around the lamb chops to coat.
6. Keep them in the fridge and marinate for at least 30 minutes, up to overnight.
7. Place the chops in the Air Fryer Basket and spray them with cooking oil.
8. Place the Air Fryer Basket again in the Air Fryer and cook for 27 minutes.
9. Press the START/PAUSE BUTTON to begin cooking.
10. Flip the chops once cooked halfway through, and resume cooking.
11. Switch the Air fryer to AIR broil mode and cook for 5 minutes.
12. Serve warm.

Serving Suggestion: Serve the chops with a dollop of cream cheese dip on top.

Variation Tip: Rub the lamb chops with balsamic vinegar or honey before seasoning.

Nutrition:

CALORIES 264 | FAT 17G |SODIUM 129MG | CARBS 0.9G | FIBER 0.3G | SUGAR 0G | PROTEIN 27G

LAMB SHANK WITH MUSHROOM SAUCE

 PREPARATION TIME
15 MINUTES

 COOKING TIME
35 MINUTES

 SERVINGS
4 PERSONS

INGREDIENTS:

- 20 mushrooms, chopped
- 2 red bell pepper, chopped
- 2 red onion, chopped
- 1 cup red wine
- 4 leeks, chopped
- 6 tablespoons balsamic vinegar
- 2 teaspoons black pepper
- 2 teaspoons salt
- 3 tablespoons fresh rosemary
- 6 garlic cloves
- 4 lamb shanks
- 3 tablespoons olive oil

PREPARATIONS:

1. Preheat your Air Fryer to 390°F using Air Fry mode.
2. Season the lamb shanks with salt, pepper, rosemary, and 1 teaspoon of olive oil.
3. Set the shanks in the Air Fryer Basket.
4. Place the Air Fryer Basket again in the Air Fryer and cook for 25 minutes.
5. Press the START/PAUSE BUTTON to begin cooking.
6. Flip the shanks halfway through, and resume cooking.
7. Meanwhile, add and heat the remaining olive oil in a skillet.
8. Add onion and garlic to sauté for 5 minutes.
9. Add in mushrooms and cook for 5 minutes.
10. Add red wine and cook until it is absorbed 11. Stir all the remaining vegetables along with black pepper and salt.
11. Cook until vegetables are al dente.
12. Serve the air-fried shanks with sautéed vegetable fry.

Serving Suggestion: Serve with sautéed zucchini and green beans.

Variation Tip: Rub the lamb shanks with lemon juice before seasoning.

Nutrition:

CALORIES 352 | FAT 9.1G |SODIUM 1294MG | CARBS 3.9G | FIBER 1G | SUGAR 1G | PROTEIN 61G

HAM BURGER PATTIES

 **PREPARATION TIME** 15 MINUTES  **COOKING TIME** 16 MINUTES  **SERVINGS** 2 PERSONS

INGREDIENTS:

- 1-pound ground beef
- Salt and pepper, to taste
- ½ teaspoon red chili powder
- ¼ teaspoon coriander powder
- 2 tablespoons chopped onion
- 1 green chili, chopped
- Oil spray for greasing
- 2 large potato wedges

PREPARATIONS:

1. Take out the rack and oil greases the air fryer basket with oil spray.
2. Add potato wedges to the basket.
3. Put the rack on top and cover it with aluminum foil.
4. Take a bowl and add minced beef in it and add salt, pepper, chili powder, coriander powder, green chili, and chopped onion.
5. Mix well and make two burger patties with wet hands.
6. Put the patties beside wedges inside the air fryer.
7. Now, set time for 12 minutes using AIR FRY mode at 400 degrees F.
8. Once the time of cooking is complete, take out the basket.
9. Flip the patties and turn and twist the potato wedges.
10. Again, set the air fryer for 4 minutes at 400 degrees F.
11. Once it's done, serve and enjoy.

Serving Suggestion: Serve it with bread slices, cheese, and pickles, lettuce, and onion.
Variation Tip: None.

Nutrition:

CALORIES875 | FAT21.5G | SODIUM 622MG | CARBS 88G | FIBER10.9 G| SUGAR 3.4G | PROTEIN 78.8G

BELL PEPPERS WITH SAUSAGES

 **PREPARATION TIME**
15 MINUTES

 **COOKING TIME**
15 MINUTES

 SERVINGS
4 PERSONS

INGREDIENTS:

- 6 beef or pork Italian sausages
- 4 bell peppers, whole
- Oil spray, for greasing
- 2 cups cooked rice
- 1 cup sour cream

PREPARATIONS:

1. Preheat the unit by selecting AIR FRY mode for 2 minutes at 325 degrees F.
2. Press START/PAUSE to start the preheating process.
3. Once preheating is done, press START/PAUSE.
4. Put the bell pepper inside the basket and sausages accommodating aside.
5. Now, place the basket inside the unit.
6. Set it to AIR FRY mode for 15 minutes at 400 degrees F.
7. Once done and serve over cooked rice with a dollop of sour cream.

Serving Suggestion: Serve it with salad.

Variation Tip: Use olive oil instead of oil spray.

Nutrition:

CALORIES1356 | FAT 81.2G| SODIUM 3044 MG | CARBS 96G | FIBER 3.1G | SUGAR 8.3G | PROTEIN 57.2 G

PARMESAN PORK CHOPS

 **PREPARATION TIME**
10 MINUTES

 **COOKING TIME**
15 MINUTES

 **SERVINGS**
4 PERSONS

INGREDIENTS:

- 4 boneless pork chops
- 2 tablespoons olive oil
- ½ cup freshly grated Parmesan
- 1 teaspoon salt
- 1 teaspoon paprika
- 1 teaspoon garlic powder
- 1 teaspoon onion powder
- ½ teaspoon black pepper

PREPARATIONS:

1. Preheat your Air Fryer to 390°F using Air Fry mode.
2. Pat dry the pork chops with a paper towel and rub them with olive oil.
3. Mix parmesan with spices in a medium bowl.
4. Rub the pork chops with Parmesan mixture.
5. Place the seasoned pork chops in the Air Fryer Basket.
6. Place the Air Fryer Basket again in the Air Fryer and cook for 15 minutes.
7. Press the START/PAUSE BUTTON to begin cooking.
8. Flip the pork chops when cooked halfway through, then resume cooking.
9. Serve warm.

Serving Suggestion: Serve boiled rice or steamed cauliflower rice.

Variation Tip: Rub the chops with garlic cloves before seasoning.

Nutrition:

CALORIES 396 | FAT 23.2G |SODIUM 622MG | CARBS 0.7G | FIBER 0G | SUGAR 0G | PROTEIN 45.6G

SHORT RIBS & ROOT VEGETABLES

 **PREPARATION TIME**
15 MINUTES

 **COOKING TIME**
45 MINUTES

 SERVINGS
2 PERSONS

INGREDIENTS:

- 1-pound beef short ribs, bone-in and trimmed
- Salt and black pepper, to taste
- 2 tablespoons canola oil, divided
- ¼ cup red wine
- 3 tablespoons brown sugar
- 2 cloves garlic, peeled, minced
- 4 carrots, peeled, cut into 1-inch pieces
- 2 parsnips, peeled, cut into 1-inch pieces
- ½ cup pearl onions

PREPARATIONS:

1. Preheat the unit by selecting AIR FRY mode for 5 minutes at 325 degrees F.
2. Press START/PAUSE to start the preheating process.
3. Once preheating is done, press START/PAUSE.
4. Season the ribs with salt and black pepper and rub a little amount of canola oil on both sides.
5. Place it in the basket of the air fryer.
6. Next, take a bowl and add pearl onions, parsnip, carrots, garlic, brown sugar, red wine, salt, and black pepper.
7. Add the vegetable mixture over the ribs.
8. Set the time to 45 minutes at 390 degrees F on AIR FRY mode.
9. Press START/PAUSE to being the cooking cycle.
10. Once the cooking is complete, take out the ingredient and serve short ribs with the mixed vegetables and liquid collected at the bottom of the basket.
11. Serve immediately and enjoy it hot.

Serving Suggestion: Serve it with mashed potatoes.

Variation Tip: Use olive oil instead of canola oil.

Nutrition:

CALORIES1262 | FAT 98.6G| SODIUM 595MG | CARBS 57G | FIBER 10.1G| SUGAR 28.2G | PROTEIN 35.8G

CHINESE BBQ PORK

 **PREPARATION TIME**
15 MINUTES

 **COOKING TIME**
25-40 MINUTES

 **SERVINGS**
2 PERSONS

INGREDIENTS:

- 4 tablespoons soy sauce
- ¼ cup red wine
- 2 tablespoons oyster sauce
- ¼ tablespoons hoisin sauce
- ¼ cup honey
- ¼ cup brown sugar
- 1 Pinch salt
- 1 Pinch black pepper
- 1 teaspoon ginger-garlic, paste
- 1 teaspoon five-spice powder

Other Ingredients
- 1.5 pounds pork shoulder, sliced

PREPARATIONS:

1. Take a bowl and mix all the ingredients listed under sauce ingredients.
2. Transfer half of it to the saucepan and let it cook for 10 minutes.
3. Set it aside.
4. Let the pork marinate in the remaining sauce for 2 hours.
5. Afterward, put the pork slices in the basket and set it to AIR FRY mode 400 degrees F for 30 minutes.
6. Make sure the internal temperature is above 160 degrees F once cooked.
7. If not, add a few more minutes to the overall cooking time.
8. Once done, take it out and baste it with prepared sauce.
9. Serve and Enjoy.

Serving Suggestion: Serve it with rice.
Variation Tip: Skip the wine and add vinegar.

Nutrition:

CALORIES 1239| FAT 73 G| SODIUM 2185 MG | CARBS 57.3 G | FIBER 0.4G | SUGAR 53.7 G | PROTEIN 81.5 G

PORK CHOPS

 **PREPARATION TIME**
10 MINUTES

 **COOKING TIME**
20 MINUTES

 **SERVINGS**
2 PERSONS

INGREDIENTS:

- 1 tablespoon rosemary, chopped
- Salt and black pepper, to taste
- 2 garlic cloves
- 1-inch ginger
- 2 tablespoons olive oil
- 8 pork chops

PREPARATIONS:

1. Take a blender and pulse together rosemary, salt, pepper, garlic cloves, ginger, and olive oil.
2. Rub this marinade over pork chops and let it rest for 1 hour.
3. Then adjust it inside the air fryer and set it to AIR FRY mode for 20minutes at 375 degrees F.
4. Once the cooking cycle is done, take out and serve hot.

Serving Suggestion: Serve it with salad.

Variation Tip: Use canola oil instead of olive oil.

Nutrition:

CALORIES 1154| FAT 93.8G| SODIUM 225MG | CARBS 2.1G | FIBER0.8 G| SUGAR 0G | PROTEIN 72.2G

STEAK AND MASHED CREAMY POTATOES

 PREPARATION TIME
15 MINUTES

 COOKING TIME
45-50 MINUTES

 SERVINGS
1 PERSONS

INGREDIENTS:

- 2 Russet potatoes, peeled and cubed
- ¼ cup butter, divided
- ⅓ cup heavy cream
- ½ cup shredded cheddar cheese
- Salt and black pepper, to taste
- 1 New York strip steak, about a pound
- 1 teaspoon olive oil
- Oil spray, for greasing

PREPARATIONS:

1. Preheat the unit by selecting AIR FRY mode for 5 minutes at 350 degrees F.
2. Press START/PAUSE to start the preheating process.
3. Once preheating is done, press START/PAUSE.
4. Rub the potatoes with salt and a little amount of olive oil about a teaspoon.
5. Next, season the steak with salt and black pepper.
6. Place the russet potatoes along with steak in the basket of the air fryer.
7. Oil sprays the steak and set it to AIR FRY mode for 50 minutes, at 375
8. degrees F.
9. Hit START/PAUSE and let the Ninja Foodi do its magic.
10. One 12 minutes pass, take out the steak and let the cooking cycle complete
11. Afterward take out potatoes and mash the potatoes and then add butter, heavy cream, and cheese along with salt and black pepper.
12. Serve the mashed potatoes with steak.
13. Enjoy.

Serving Suggestion: Serve it with rice.
Variation Tip: Use Parmesan instead of cheddar.

Nutrition:

CALORIES1932 | FAT 85.2G| SODIUM 3069MG | CARBS 82G | FIBER10.3 G| SUGAR 5.3G | PROTEIN 22.5G

STEAK IN AIR FRY

 **PREPARATION TIME**
15 MINUTES

 **COOKING TIME**
22 MINUTES

 **SERVINGS**
1 PERSONS

INGREDIENTS:

- 2 teaspoons canola oil
- 1 tablespoon Montreal steaks seasoning
- 1-pound beef steak

PREPARATIONS:

1. Season the steak on both sides with canola oil and then rub a generous amount of steak seasoning all over.
2. Put the steak in the basket and set it to AIR FRY mode at 400 degrees F for 22 minutes.
3. After 7 minutes, hit pause and take out the basket to flip the steak and cover it with foil on top, for the remaining 14 minutes.
4. Once done, serve the medium-rare steak and enjoy it by resting for 10 minutes.
5. Serve by cutting in slices.
6. Enjoy.

Serving Suggestion: Serve it with mashed potatoes.
Variation Tip: Use vegetable oil instead of canola oil.

Nutrition:

CALORIES 935 | FAT 37.2G | SODIUM 1419MG | CARBS 0G | FIBER 0G | SUGAR 0G | PROTEIN 137.5 G

BEEF RIBS I

 **PREPARATION TIME**
10 MINUTES

 **COOKING TIME**
18 MINUTES

 **SERVINGS**
2 PERSONS

INGREDIENTS:

- 4 tablespoons barbecue spice rub
- 1 tablespoon kosher salt and black pepper
- 3 tablespoons brown sugar
- 2 pounds beef ribs (3-3 ½ pounds), cut in thirds
- 1 cup barbecue sauce

PREPARATIONS:

1. In a small bowl, add salt, pepper, brown sugar, and BBQ spice rub.
2. Grease the ribs with oil spray from both sides and then rub them with a spice mixture.
3. Adjust the ribs inside the Ninja Air Fryer, and set it to AIR FRY mode at 375 degrees F for 18 minutes.
4. Hit START/PAUSE and let the air fryer cook the ribs.
5. Once done, serve with the BBQ sauce.

Serving Suggestion: Serve it with salad and baked potato.

Variation Tip: Use sea salt instead of kosher salt.

Nutrition:

CALORIES1081 | FAT 28.6 G| SODIUM 1701MG | CARBS 58G | FIBER 0.8G| SUGAR 45.7G | PROTEIN 138 G

BEEF RIBS II

 **PREPARATION TIME**
20 MINUTES

 **COOKING TIME**
60 MINUTES

 **SERVINGS**
2 PERSONS

INGREDIENTS:

Marinade
- ¼ cup olive oil
- 4 garlic cloves, minced
- ½ cup white wine vinegar
- ¼ cup soy sauce, reduced-sodium
- ¼ cup Worcestershire sauce
- 1 lemon juice
- Salt and black pepper, to taste
- 2 tablespoons Italian seasoning
- 1 teaspoon smoked paprika
- 2 tablespoons mustard
- ½ cup maple syrup

Meat Ingredients
- Oil spray, for greasing
- 8 beef ribs lean

PREPARATIONS:

1. Preheat the unit by selecting AIR FRY mode for 2 minutes at 325 degrees F.
2. Press START/PAUSE to start the preheating process.
3. Once preheating is done, press START/PAUSE.
4. Take a large bowl and add all the ingredients under marinade ingredients.
5. Put the marinade in a zip lock bag and add ribs to it.
6. Let it sit for 4 hours.
7. Now take out the basket of the air fryer and grease the basket with oil spray.
8. Now put the ribs in the basket.
9. Set it to AIR FRY mode at 220 degrees F for 30 minutes.
10. Select Pause and take out the basket.
11. Afterward, flip the ribs and cook for 30 more minutes at 250 degrees F.
12. Once done, serve the juicy and tender ribs.
13. Enjoy.

Serving Suggestion: Serve it with Mac and cheese.

Variation Tip: Use garlic-infused oil instead of garlic cloves.

Nutrition:

CALORIES 1927| FAT 116G| SODIUM 1394MG | CARBS 35.2G | FIBER 1.3G | SUGAR 29G | PROTEIN 172.3G

POULTRY

CRUSTED CHICKEN BREAST

 **PREPARATION TIME**
15 MINUTES

 **COOKING TIME**
28 MINUTES

 **SERVINGS**
4 PERSONS

Ingredients:

- 2 large eggs, beaten
- ½ cup all-purpose flour
- 1 ¼ cups panko bread crumbs
- ⅔ cup Parmesan, grated
- 4 teaspoons lemon zest
- 2 teaspoons dried oregano
- Salt, to taste
- 1 teaspoon cayenne pepper
- Freshly black pepper, to taste
- 4 boneless skinless chicken breasts

Preparations:

1. Preheat your Air Fryer to 390°F using Air Fry mode.
2. Beat eggs in one shallow bowl and spread flour in another shallow bowl.
3. Mix panko with oregano, lemon zest, Parmesan, cayenne, oregano, salt, and black pepper in another shallow bowl.
4. First, coat the chicken with flour first, then dip it in the eggs and coat them with panko mixture.
5.
6. Arrange the prepared chicken in the Air Fryer Basket.
7. Place the Air Fryer Basket again in the Air Fryer and cook for 28 minutes.
8. Press the START/PAUSE BUTTON to begin cooking.
9. Flip the half-cooked chicken and continue cooking until golden.
10. Serve warm.

Serving Suggestion: Serve with fresh-cut tomatoes and sautéed greens.

Variation Tip: Rub the chicken with lemon juice before seasoning.

Nutrition:

CALORIES 220 | FAT 13G |SODIUM 542MG | CARBS 0.9G | FIBER 0.3G | SUGAR 0.2G | PROTEIN 25.6G

BALSAMIC DUCK BREAST

 **PREPARATION TIME**
15 MINUTES

 **COOKING TIME**
20 MINUTES

 **SERVINGS**
2 PERSONS

Ingredients:

- 2 Duck Breasts
- 1 teaspoon parsley
- Salt and black pepper, to taste
- Marinade:
- 1 tablespoon olive oil
- ½ teaspoon French mustard
- 1 teaspoon dried garlic
- 2 teaspoons honey
- ½ teaspoon balsamic vinegar

Preparations:

1. Preheat your Air Fryer to 390°F using Air Fry mode.
2. Mix olive oil, mustard, garlic, honey, and balsamic vinegar in a bowl.
3. Add duck breasts to the marinade and rub well.
4. Place one duck breast in the Air Fryer Basket.
5. Place the Air Fryer Basket again in the Air Fryer and cook for 20 minutes.
6. Press the START/PAUSE BUTTON to begin cooking.
7. Flip the duck breasts once cooked halfway through, then resume cooking.
8. Serve warm.

Serving Suggestion: Serve with white rice and avocado salad
Variation Tip: Rub the duck breast with garlic cloves before seasoning.

Nutrition:

CALORIES 546 | FAT 33.1G |SODIUM 1201MG | CARBS 30G | FIBER 2.4G | SUGAR 9.7G | PROTEIN 32G

CHICKEN WINGS

 **PREPARATION TIME** 15 MINUTES    **COOKING TIME** 20 MINUTES    **SERVINGS** 3 PERSONS

Ingredients:

- 1 cup chicken batter mix, Louisiana
- 9 Chicken wings
- ½ teaspoon smoked paprika
- 2 tablespoons Dijon mustard
- 1 tablespoon cayenne pepper
- 1 teaspoon meat tenderizer, powder
- Oil spray, for greasing

Preparations:

1. Pat dry chicken wings, and add mustard, paprika, meat tenderizer, and cayenne pepper.
2. Dredge it in the chicken batter mix.
3. Oil sprays the chicken wings.
4. Grease the basket of the air fryer.
5. Put the wings into the air fryer.
6. Set it to AIR FRY mode at 400 degrees F for 20 minutes 7. Hit START/PAUSE to begin with the cooking.
7. Once the cooking cycle is complete, serve, and enjoy hot.

Serving Suggestion: Serve it with salad.

Variation Tip: Use American yellow mustard instead of Dijon mustard.

Nutrition:

CALORIES621 | FAT 32.6G| SODIUM 2016MG | CARBS 46.6G | FIBER 1.1G | SUGAR 0.2G | PROTEIN 32.1G

PICKLED CHICKEN FILLETS

 **PREPARATION TIME**
15 MINUTES

 **COOKING TIME**
28 MINUTES

 **SERVINGS**
4 PERSONS

Ingredients:

- 2 boneless chicken breasts
- ½ cup dill pickle juice
- 2 eggs
- ½ cup milk
- 1 cup flour, all-purpose
- 2 tablespoons powdered sugar
- 2 tablespoons potato starch
- 1 teaspoon paprika
- 1 teaspoon of sea salt
- ½ teaspoon black pepper
- ½ teaspoon garlic powder
- ¼ teaspoon ground celery seed ground
- 1 tablespoon olive oil
- Cooking spray
- 4 hamburger buns, toasted
- 8 dill pickle chips

Preparations:

1. Preheat your Air Fryer to 390°F using Air Fry mode.
2. Set the chicken in a suitable Ziploc bag and pound it into ½ thickness with a mallet.
3. Slice the chicken into 2 halves.
4. Add pickle juice and seal the bag.
5. Refrigerate for 30 minutes approximately for marination. Whisk both eggs with milk in a shallow bowl.
6. Thoroughly mix flour with spices and flour in a separate bowl.
7. Dip each chicken slice in egg, then in the flour mixture.
8. Shake off the excess and set the chicken pieces in the Air Fryer Basket.
9. Spray the pieces with cooking oil.
10. Place the chicken pieces in the Air Fryer Basket in a single layer and spray the cooking oil.
11. Place the Air Fryer Basket again in the Air Fryer and cook for 28 minutes.
12. Press the START/PAUSE BUTTON to begin cooking.
13. Flip the chicken pieces once cooked halfway through, and resume cooking.
14. Enjoy with pickle chips and a dollop of mayonnaise.

Serving Suggestion: Serve with warm corn tortilla and Greek salad.

Variation Tip: You can use the almond flour breading for a low-carb serving.

Nutrition:

CALORIES 353 | FAT 5G |SODIUM 818MG | CARBS 53.2G | FIBER 4.4G | SUGAR 8G | PROTEIN 17.3G

CHILI CHICKEN WINGS

 **PREPARATION TIME**
20 MINUTES

 **COOKING TIME**
43 MINUTES

 **SERVINGS**
4 PERSONS

Ingredients:

- 8 chicken wings drumettes
- cooking spray
- ⅛ cup low-fat buttermilk
- ¼ cup almond flour
- McCormick chicken seasoning to taste

Thai Chili Marinade

- 1 ½ tablespoon low-sodium soy sauce
- ½ teaspoon ginger, minced
- 1 ½ garlic cloves
- 1 green onion
- ½ teaspoon rice wine vinegar
- ½ tablespoon Sriracha sauce
- ½ tablespoon sesame oil

Preparations:

1. Preheat your Air Fryer to 390°F using Air Fry mode.
2. Put all the ingredients for the marinade in the blender and blend them for 1 minute.
3. Keep this marinade aside. Pat dry the washed chicken and place it in the Ziploc bag.
4. Add buttermilk, chicken seasoning, and zip the bag.
5. Shake the bag well, then refrigerator for 30 minutes for marination.
6. Remove the chicken drumettes from the marinade, then dredge them through dry flour.
7. Spread the drumettes in the Air Fryer Basket and spray them with cooking oil.
8. Place the Air Fryer Basket again in the Air Fryer and cook for 43 minutes.
9. Press the START/PAUSE BUTTON to begin cooking.
10. Toss the drumettes once cooked halfway through.
11. Now brush the chicken pieces with Thai chili sauce and then resume cooking.
12. Serve warm.

Serving Suggestion: Serve with warm corn tortilla and ketchup.

Variation Tip: Rub the wings with lemon or orange juice before cooking.

Nutrition:

CALORIES 223 | FAT 11.7G |SODIUM 721MG | CARBS 13.6G | FIBER 0.7G | SUGAR 8G | PROTEIN 15.7G

SWEET AND SPICY CARROTS WITH CHICKEN THIGHS

 **PREPARATION TIME**
15 MINUTES

 **COOKING TIME**
25 MINUTES

 **SERVINGS**
2 PERSONS

Ingredients:

Glaze
- Cooking spray, for greasing
- 2 tablespoons butter, melted
- 1 tablespoon hot honey
- 1 teaspoon orange zest
- 1 teaspoon cardamom
- ½ pound baby carrots
- 1 tablespoon orange juice
- Salt and black pepper, to taste

Other Ingredients
- ½ pound carrots, baby carrots
- 8 chicken thighs

Preparations:

1. Take a bowl and mix all the glaze ingredients in it.
2. Now, coat the chicken and carrots with the glaze and let them rest for 30 minutes.
3. Now place the chicken thighs and carrots into the air fryer basket.
4. Press start and set it to ROAST mode at 390 degrees F for 25 minutes.
5. After 12 minutes, take out the carrots and let the cooking cycle complete for the chicken.
6. Then serve it hot.

Serving Suggestion: Serve with Salad.
Variation Tip: Use lime juice instead of orange juice.

Nutrition:

CALORIES 1312| FAT 55.4G| SODIUM 757MG | CARBS 23.3G | FIBER6.7 G | SUGAR12 G | PROTEIN171 G

CHICKEN LEG PIECE

 **PREPARATION TIME**
15 MINUTES

 **COOKING TIME**
25 MINUTES

 **SERVINGS**
1 PERSONS

Ingredients:

- 1 teaspoon onion powder
- 1 teaspoon paprika powder
- 1 teaspoon garlic powder
- Salt and black pepper, to taste
- 1 tablespoon Italian seasoning
- 1 teaspoon celery seeds
- 2 eggs, whisked
- ⅓ cup buttermilk
- 1 cornflour
- 1-pound chicken leg

Preparations:

1. Take a bowl and whisk egg along with pepper, salt, and buttermilk.
2. Set it aside for further use.
3. Mix all the spices in a small separate bowl.
4. Dredge the chicken in egg wash then dredge it in seasoning.
5. Coat the chicken legs with oil spray.
6. At the end, dust it with cornflour.
7. Put the leg pieces into the air fryer basket.
8. Set it to 400 degrees F, for 25 minutes.
9. Let the air fryer do the magic.
10. Once it's done, serve and enjoy.

Serving Suggestion: Serve it with cooked rice.
Variation Tip: Use water instead of buttermilk.

Nutrition:

CALORIES 1511| FAT 52.3G| SODIUM615 MG | CARBS 100G | FIBER 9.2G | SUGAR 8.1G | PROTEIN 154.2G

YUMMY CHICKEN BREASTS

 **PREPARATION TIME**
15 MINUTES

 COOKING TIME
25 MINUTES

 SERVINGS
2 PERSONS

Ingredients:

- 4 large chicken breasts, 6 ounces each
- 2 tablespoons oil bay seasoning
- 1 tablespoon Montreal chicken seasoning
- 1 teaspoon thyme
- ½ teaspoon paprika
- Salt, to taste
- Oil spray, for greasing

Preparations:

1. Season the chicken breast pieces with the listed seasoning and let them rest for 40 minutes.
2. Grease both sides of the chicken breast pieces with oil spray.
3. Put the chicken breast pieces inside the basket.
4. Set the AIR FRY mode at 400 degrees F, for 15 minutes.
5. Select pause and take out the basket and flip the chicken breast pieces, after 15 minutes.
6. Select AIR FRY at 400 degrees F, for 10 more minutes.
7. Once it's done serve.

Serving Suggestion: Serve it with a baked potato.

Variation Tip: None

Nutrition:

CALORIES 711| FAT 27.7G| SODIUM 895MG | CARBS 1.6G | FIBER 0.4G | SUGAR 0.1G | PROTEIN 106.3G

SPICED CHICKEN AND VEGETABLES

 PREPARATION TIME
22 MINUTES

 COOKING TIME
35 MINUTES

 SERVINGS
1 PERSONS

Ingredients:

- 2 large chicken breasts
- 2 teaspoons olive oil
- 1 teaspoon chili powder
- 1 teaspoon paprika powder
- 1 teaspoon onion powder
- ½ teaspoon garlic powder
- ¼ teaspoon Cumin
- Salt and black pepper, to taste

Vegetable Ingredients

- 2 large potatoes, cubed
- 4 large carrots cut into bite-size pieces
- 1 tablespoon olive oil
- Salt and black pepper, to taste

Preparations:

1. Take chicken breast pieces and rub olive oil, salt, pepper, chili powder, onion powder, cumin, garlic powder, and paprika.
2. Season the vegetables with olive oil, salt, and black pepper.
3. Now put the chicken breast pieces along with vegetables inside the air fryer basket.
4. Now set it to AIR FRY mode at 390 degrees F, for 35 minutes.
5. Once the cooking cycle is done, serve, and enjoy.

Serving Suggestion: Serve it with salad or ranch dressing.

Variation Tip: Use Canola oil instead of olive oil.

Nutrition:

CALORIES1510 | FAT 51.3G| SODIUM 525MG | CARBS 163G | FIBER24.7 G | SUGAR 21.4G | PROTEIN 102.9

CHICKEN BREAST STRIPS

PREPARATION TIME
10 MINUTES

COOKING TIME
22 MINUTES

SERVINGS
2 PERSONS

Ingredients:

- 2 large organic egg
- 1-ounce buttermilk
- 1 cup cornmeal
- ¼ cup all-purpose flour
- Salt and black pepper, to taste
- 1-pound chicken breasts, cut into strips
- 2 tablespoons oil bay seasoning
- Oil spray, for greasing

Preparations:

1. Take a medium bowl and whisk eggs with buttermilk.
2. In a separate large bowl, mix flour, cornmeal, salt, black pepper, and oil bay seasoning.
3. First, dip the chicken breast strip in egg wash and then dredge into the flour mixture.
4. Coat the strip all over and layer it inside the basket that is already greased with oil spray.
5. Grease the chicken breast strips with oil spray as well.
6. Set the basket to AIR FRY mode at 400 degrees F for 22 minutes.
7. Hit the START/PAUSE button to let the cooking start.
8. Once the cooking cycle is done, serve.

Serving Suggestion: Serve it with roasted vegetables.

Variation Tip: None

Nutrition:

CALORIES 788 | FAT 25G | SODIUM 835 MG | CARBS 60G | FIBER 4.9G | SUGAR 1.5G | PROTEIN 79G

CORNISH HEN WITH ASPARAGUS

 PREPARATION TIME
20 MINUTES

 COOKING TIME
45 MINUTES

 SERVINGS
2 PERSONS

Ingredients:

- 10 spears asparagus
- Salt and black pepper, to taste
- 1 Cornish hen
- Salt, to taste
- Black pepper, to taste
- 1 teaspoon Paprika
- Coconut spray, for greasing
- 2 lemons, sliced

Preparations:

1. Wash and pat dry the asparagus and coat it with coconut oil spray.
2. Sprinkle salt on the asparagus and place it inside the bottom of the basket of the air fryer.
3. Next, take the Cornish hen and rub it well with salt, black pepper, and paprika.
4. Spray the Cornish hen with oil and place it on top of asparagus inside the air fryer basket.
5. Set the time to 45 minutes at 350 degrees F, by selecting the ROAST mode.
6. Once the 6 minutes pass hit the START/PAUSE button and take out the asparagus.
7. Put the basket back in the unit.
8. Once the chicken cooking cycle is complete, transfer the chicken to the serving plate.
9. Serve the chicken with roasted asparagus and slices of lemon.
10. Serve hot and enjoy.

Serving Suggestion: Serve it with ranch dressing.
Variation Tip: You can add variation by choosing chopped cilantro instead of a lemon slice.

Nutrition:

CALORIES 192| FAT 4.7G| SODIUM 151MG | CARBS10.7 G | FIBER 4.6G | SUGAR 3.8G | PROTEIN 30G

VEGETABLES

GARLIC POTATO WEDGES IN AIR FRYER

 **PREPARATION TIME** 10 MINUTES

 **COOKING TIME** 20 MINUTES

 **SERVINGS** 2 PERSONS

Ingredients:

- 4 medium potatoes, peeled and cut into wedges
- 4 tablespoons butter
- 1 teaspoon chopped cilantro
- 1 cup plain flour
- 1 teaspoon garlic, minced
- Salt and black pepper, to taste

Preparations:

1. Soak the potato wedges for 30 minutes in cold water.
2. Drain and pat dry with a paper towel after that.
3. Bring a big saucepan of water to a boil, then cook the wedges for 3 minutes.
4. Finally, drain it on a paper towel.
5. In a mixing bowl, stir together the garlic, melted butter, salt, pepper, and cilantro.
6. In a separate basin, combine the flour, salt, and black pepper.
7. Finally, add enough water to the flour to make it runny.
8. Toss the potatoes in the flour mixture and place them in a foil baking pan.
9. In the air fryer basket, place the foil tin.
10. Now set the timer for 20 minutes at 390 degrees F using the AIR FRY mode.
11. When everything is ready, serve and enjoy.

Serving Suggestion: Serve with ketchup.

Variation Tip: Use olive oil instead of butter.

Nutrition:

CALORIES 727 | FAT 24.1G | SODIUM 191MG | CARBS 115.1G | FIBER 12G | SUGAR 5.1G | PROTEIN14 G

CURLY FRIES

 **PREPARATION TIME**
10 MINUTES

 **COOKING TIME**
20 MINUTES

 **SERVINGS**
6 PERSONS

Ingredients:

- 2 spiralized zucchinis
- 1 cup flour
- 2 tablespoons paprika
- 1 teaspoon cayenne pepper
- 1 teaspoon garlic powder
- 1 teaspoon black pepper
- 1 teaspoon salt
- 2 eggs
- Olive oil or cooking spray

Preparations:

1. Preheat your Air Fryer to 390°F using Air Fry mode.
2. In a mixing bowl, combine flour, paprika, cayenne pepper, garlic powder, black pepper, and salt.
3. In a separate bowl, beat the eggs and dip the zucchini in them.
4. Place the zucchini in the Air Fryer Basket after coating it with the flour mixture.
5. Drizzle some frying oil over the zucchini.
6. Return the Air Fryer Basket to the Air Fryer and cook for an additional 20 minutes.
7. To begin cooking, press the START/PAUSE BUTTON.
8. Toss the zucchini halfway through cooking and continue to cook.
9. Serve immediately.

Serving Suggestion: Serve with red chunky salsa or chili sauce.

Variation Tip: Use crushed cornflakes for breading to have extra crispiness.

Nutrition:

CALORIES 212 | FAT 11.8G |SODIUM 321MG | CARBS 24.6G | FIBER 4.4G | SUGAR 8G | PROTEIN 7.3G

FRIED OLIVES

 **PREPARATION TIME**
15 MINUTES

 **COOKING TIME**
9 MINUTES

 **SERVINGS**
6 PERSONS

Ingredients:

- 2 cups blue cheese stuffed olives, drained
- ½ cup all-purpose flour
- 1 cup panko breadcrumbs
- ½ teaspoon garlic powder
- 1 pinch oregano
- 2 eggs

Preparations:

1. Preheat your Air Fryer to 390°F using Air Fry mode.
2. Mix flour with oregano and garlic powder in a bowl and beat two eggs in another bowl.
3. Spread panko breadcrumbs in a bowl.
4. Coat all the olives with the flour mixture, dip in the eggs and then coat with the panko breadcrumbs.
5. As you coat the olives, place them in the Air Fryer Basket in a single layer, then spray them with cooking oil.
6. Place the Air Fryer Basket again in the Air Fryer and cook for 9 minutes.
7. Press the START/PAUSE BUTTON to begin cooking.
8. Flip the olives once cooked halfway through, then resume cooking.
9. Serve.

Serving Suggestion: Serve with red chunky salsa or chili sauce.

Variation Tip: Use crushed cornflakes for breading to have extra crispiness.

Nutrition:

CALORIES 166 | FAT 3.2G | SODIUM 437MG | CARBS 28.8G | FIBER 1.8G | SUGAR 2.7G | PROTEIN 5.8G

QUINOA PATTIES

 **PREPARATION TIME**
15 MINUTES

 **COOKING TIME**
32 MINUTES

 **SERVINGS**
4 PERSONS

Ingredients:

- 1 cup quinoa red
- 1½ cups water
- 1 teaspoon salt
- black pepper, ground
- 1½ cups rolled oats
- 3 eggs beaten
- ¼ cup minced white onion
- ½ cup crumbled feta cheese
- ¼ cup chopped fresh chives
- Salt and black pepper, to taste
- Vegetable or canola oil
- 4 hamburger buns
- 4 arugulas
- 4 slices tomato sliced
- Cucumber yogurt dill sauce
- 1 cup cucumber, diced
- 1 cup Greek yogurt
- 2 teaspoons lemon juice
- ¼ teaspoon salt
- Black pepper, ground
- 1 tablespoon chopped fresh dill
- 1 tablespoon olive oil

Preparations:

1. Preheat your Air Fryer to 390°F using Air Fry mode.
2. Place the quinoa in a saucepan with cold water, salt, and black pepper over medium-high heat.
3. Bring the quinoa to a boil, then reduce ta low heat, cover, and simmer for 20 minutes.
4. Remove the cooked quinoa from the heat and fluff and mix it with a fork.
5. Place the quinoa in a baking dish and spread it out evenly.
6. Combine eggs, oats, onion, herbs, cheese, salt, and black pepper in a large mixing bowl.
7. Add the quinoa and mix thoroughly. This quinoa cheese combination should yield 4 burgers.
8. Spray the patties with cooking oil and place them in the Air Fryer Basket.
9. Return the Air Fryer Basket to the Air Fryer and cook for an additional 13 minutes.
10. To begin cooking, press the START/PAUSE BUTTON.
11. Flip the patties once cooked halfway through, and resume cooking.
12. Meanwhile, prepare the cucumber yogurt dill sauce by mixing all of its ingredients in a mixing bowl.
13. Place each quinoa patty in a burger bun along with arugula leaves.
14. Serve with yogurt dill sauce.

Serving Suggestion: Serve with yogurt dip.
Variation Tip: Use crushed cornflakes for breading to have extra crispiness.

Nutrition:

CALORIES 231 | FAT 9G | SODIUM 271MG | CARBS 32.8G | FIBER 6.4G | SUGAR 7G | PROTEIN 6.3G

SWEET POTATOES WITH HONEY BUTTER

PREPARATION TIME
15 MINUTES

COOKING TIME
40 MINUTES

SERVINGS
4 PERSONS

INGREDIENTS:

- 4 sweet potatoes, scrubbed
- 1 teaspoon oil
- Honey Butter
- 4 tablespoons unsalted butter
- 1 tablespoon honey
- 2 teaspoons hot sauce
- ¼ teaspoon salt

PREPARATIONS:

1. Preheat your Air Fryer to 390ºF using Air Fry mode.
2. Rub the sweet potatoes with oil and place two potatoes in the Air Fryer Basket.
3. Place the Air Fryer Basket again in the Air Fryer and cook for 40 minutes.
4. Press the START/PAUSE BUTTON to begin cooking.
5. Flip the potatoes once cooked halfway through, then resume cooking.
6. Mix butter with hot sauce, honey, and salt in a bowl.
7. When the potatoes are done, cut a slit on top and make a well with a spoon.
8. Pour the honey butter into each potato jacket.
9. Serve.

Serving Suggestion: Serve with sautéed vegetables and salad.

Variation Tip: Sprinkle crumbled bacon and parsley on top.

Nutrition:

CALORIES 288 | FAT 6.9G | SODIUM 761MG | CARBS 46G | FIBER 4G | SUGAR 12G | PROTEIN 9.6G

FRIED ARTICHOKE HEARTS

 **PREPARATION TIME**
15 MINUTES

 **COOKING TIME**
10 MINUTES

 SERVINGS
6 PERSONS

INGREDIENTS:

- 3 cans Quartered Artichokes, drained
- ½ cup mayonnaise
- 1 cup panko breadcrumbs
- ⅓ cup grated Parmesan
- salt and black pepper to taste
- Parsley for garnish

PREPARATIONS:

1. Preheat your Air Fryer to 390°F using Air Fry mode.
2. Combine mayonnaise, salt, and black pepper in a mixing bowl and set aside.
3. In a mixing dish, spread panko breadcrumbs.
4. Toss the breadcrumbs with the artichoke pieces.
5. Place the artichokes in a single layer in the Air Fryer Basket as you coat them, then spray them with cooking oil.
6. Return the Air Fryer Basket to the Air Fryer and cook for an additional 10 minutes.
7. To begin cooking, press the START/PAUSE BUTTON.
8. Once the artichokes are halfway cooked, flip them and continue cooking.
9. Serve warm with mayo sauce.

Serving Suggestion: Serve with red chunky salsa or chili sauce.

Variation Tip: Use crushed cornflakes for breading to have extra crispiness.

Nutrition:

CALORIES 193 | FAT 1G | SODIUM 395MG | CARBS 38.7G | FIBER 1.6G | SUGAR 0.9G | PROTEIN 6.6G

ZUCCHINI CAKES

 **PREPARATION TIME**
10 MINUTES

 COOKING TIME
32 MINUTES

 SERVINGS
6 PERSONS

Ingredients:

- 2 medium zucchinis, grated
- 1 cup corn kernel
- 1 medium potato cooked
- 2 tablespoons chickpea flour
- 2 garlic minced
- 2 teaspoons olive oil
- Salt and black pepper
- For Serving:
- Yogurt tahini sauce

Preparations:

1. Preheat your Air Fryer to 390°F using Air Fry mode.
2. In a colander, combine shredded zucchini with a pinch of salt and set aside for 15 minutes.
3. Squeeze out any excess moisture.
4. In a large mixing bowl, mash the boiled potato using a fork.
5. In a mixing dish, combine the zucchini, corn, garlic, chickpea flour, salt, and black pepper.
6. Combine the ingredients for these fritters and roll them into 2 tablespoon-sized balls, lightly flattening them.
7. Arrange the fritters in a single layer in the Air Fryer Basket and spray with cooking spray.
8. Return the Air Fryer Basket to the Air Fryer and cook for an additional 17 minutes.
9. To begin cooking, press the START/PAUSE BUTTON.
10. Once the fritters are halfway done, flip them and continue frying.
11. Serve and eat

Serving Suggestion: Serve with mayonnaise or cream cheese dip.

Variation Tip: Use crushed cornflakes for breading to have extra crispiness.

Nutrition:

CALORIES 270 | FAT 14.6G | SODIUM 394MG | CARBS 31.3G | FIBER 7.5G | SUGAR 9.7G | PROTEIN 6.4G

GREEN BEANS WITH BAKED POTATOES

 **PREPARATION TIME**
15 MINUTES

 **COOKING TIME**
45 MINUTES

 SERVINGS
2 PERSONS

Ingredients:

- 2 cups green beans
- 2 large potatoes, cubed
- 3 tablespoons olive oil
- 1 teaspoon seasoned salt
- ½ teaspoon chili powder
- ⅛ teaspoon garlic powder
- ¼ teaspoon onion powder

Preparations:

1. Pour olive oil into a large mixing bowl.
2. Whisk all of the seasonings in olive oil.
3. Toss the green bean in it and then place it in the air fryer basket.
4. Season the potatoes and toss them into the basket with the spice.
5. Now put the unit to AIR FRY mode for 45 minutes at 350 degrees F.
6. Remove the asparagus after 18 minutes and continue to cook.
7. When the cooking cycle is finished, remove the dish from the oven and transfer it to serving plates.

Serving Suggestion: Serve with rice.
Variation Tip: Use canola oil instead of olive oil.

Nutrition:

CALORIES473 | FAT21.6G | SODIUM796 MG | CARBS 66.6G | FIBER12.9 G | SUGAR6G | PROTEIN8.4 G

ZUCCHINI WITH STUFFING

 **PREPARATION TIME**
12 MINUTES

 COOKING TIME
20 MINUTES

 SERVINGS
3 PERSONS

Ingredients:

- 1 cup quinoa, rinsed
- 1 cup black olives
- 6 medium zucchinis, about 2 pounds
- 2 cups cannellini beans, drained
- 1 white onion, chopped
- ¼ cup almonds, chopped
- 4 cloves garlic, chopped
- 4 tablespoons olive oil
- 1 cup water
- 2 cups Parmesan cheese, for topping

Preparations:

1. First wash the zucchini and cut it lengthwise.
2. Take a skillet and heat oil in it.
3. Sauté the onion in olive oil for a few minutes.
4. Then add the quinoa and water and let it cook for 8 minutes with the lid on the top.
5. Transfer the quinoa to a bowl and add all remaining ingredients excluding zucchini and Parmesan cheese.
6. Scoop out the seeds of zucchinis.
7. Fill the cavity of zucchinis with a bowl mixture.
8. Top it with a handful of Parmesan cheese.
9. Arrange 4 zucchinis in the air fryer basket.
10. Select the AIR FRY for 20 minutes and adjust the temperature to 390 degrees F.
11. Once done, serve and enjoy.

Serving Suggestion: Serve it with pasta.
Variation Tip: None.

Nutrition:

CALORIES 1171 | FAT 48.6G | SODIUM 1747MG | CARBS 132.4G | FIBER 42.1G | SUGAR 11.5G | PROTEIN 65.7G

MIXED AIR FRY VEGGIES

 **PREPARATION TIME**
15 MINUTES

 **COOKING TIME**
25 MINUTES

 **SERVINGS**
4 PERSONS

Ingredients:

- 2 cups carrots, cubed
- 2 cups potatoes, cubed
- 2 cups shallots, cubed
- 2 cups zucchini, diced
- 2 cups yellow squash, cubed
- Salt and black pepper, to taste
- 1 tablespoon Italian seasoning
- 2 tablespoons ranch seasoning
- 4 tablespoons olive oil

Preparations:

1. Take a large bowl and add all the veggies to it.
2. Season the veggies with salt, pepper, Italian seasoning, ranch seasoning, and olive oil.
3. Toss all the ingredients well.
4. Now put it in the basket of the air fryer.
5. Set the unit to AIR FRY mode at 360 degrees F for 25 minutes.
6. Once it is cooked and done, serve, and enjoy.

Serving Suggestion: Serve it with rice.
Variation Tip: None.

Nutrition:

CALORIES 275 | FAT 15.3G | SODIUM 129MG | CARBS 33G | FIBER 3.8G | SUGAR 5G | PROTEIN 4.4G

AIR FRIED OKRA

 **PREPARATION TIME** 10 MINUTES    **COOKING TIME** 13 MINUTES    **SERVINGS** 2 PERSONS

Ingredients:

- ½ lb. okra pods sliced
- 1 teaspoon olive oil
- ¼ teaspoon salt
- ⅛ teaspoon black pepper

Preparations:

1. Preheat your Air Fryer to 390°F using Air Fry mode.
2. Toss okra with olive oil, salt, and black pepper in a bowl.
3. Spread the okra in a single layer in the Air Fryer Basket.
4. Place the Air Fryer Basket again in the Air Fryer and cook for 13 minutes.
5. Press the START/PAUSE BUTTON to begin cooking.
6. Toss the okra once cooked halfway through, and resume cooking.
7. Serve warm.

Serving Suggestion: Serve with potato chips and bread slices.
Variation Tip: Sprinkle cornmeal before cooking for added crispiness.

Nutrition:

CALORIES 208 | FAT 5G |SODIUM 1205MG | CARBS 34.1G | FIBER 7.8G | SUGAR 2.5G | PROTEIN 5.9G

FRESH MIX VEGGIES IN AIR FRYER

 **PREPARATION TIME**
15 MINUTES

 **COOKING TIME**
12 MINUTES

 **SERVINGS**
4 PERSONS

Ingredients:

- 1 cup cauliflower florets
- 1 cup carrots, peeled chopped
- 1 cup broccoli florets
- 2 tablespoons avocado oil
- Salt, to taste
- ½ teaspoon chili powder
- ½ teaspoon garlic powder
- ½ teaspoon herbs de Provence
- 1 cup parmesan cheese

Preparations:

1. Take a bowl, and add all the veggies to it.
2. Toss and then season the veggies with salt, chili powder, garlic powder, and herbs de Provence.
3. Toss it all well and then drizzle avocado oil.
4. Make sure the ingredients are coated well.
5. Now transfer the veggies to the basket of the air fryer.
6. Turn on the start button and set it to AIR FRY mode at 390 degrees for 10-12 minutes.
7. After 8 minutes of cooking, select the pause button and then take out the basket and sprinkle Parmesan cheese on top of the veggies.
8. Then let the cooking cycle complete for the next 3-4 minutes.
9. Once done, serve.

Serving Suggestion: Serve it with rice.

Variation Tip: Use canola oil or butter instead of avocado oil.

Nutrition:

CALORIES 161 | FAT 9.3G | SODIUM 434MG | CARBS 7.7G | FIBER 2.4G | SUGAR 2.5G | PROTEIN 13.9

KALE AND SPINACH CHIPS

 **PREPARATION TIME**
12 MINUTES

 **COOKING TIME**
8 MINUTES

 **SERVINGS**
2 PERSONS

Ingredients:

- 2 cups spinach, torn in pieces and stem removed
- 2 cups kale, torn in pieces, stems removed
- 1 tablespoon olive oil
- Sea salt, to taste
- ⅓ cup Parmesan cheese

Preparations:

1. Take a bowl and add spinach to it.
2. Take another bowl and add kale to it.
3. Now, season both of them with olive oil, and sea salt.
4. Add kale and spinach to the basket of the air fryer.
5. Select the AIR FRY mode at 350 degrees F for 8 minutes.
6. Once done, take out the crispy chips and sprinkle Parmesan cheese on top.
7. Serve and Enjoy.

Serving Suggestion: Serve it with baked potato.
Variation Tip: Use canola oil instead of olive oil.

Nutrition:

CALORIES 166| FAT 11.1G| SODIUM 355MG | CARBS 8.1G | FIBER 1.7G | SUGAR 0.1G | PROTEIN 8.2G

BRUSSELS SPROUTS

 **PREPARATION TIME** 15 MINUTES

 **COOKING TIME** 20 MINUTES

 **SERVINGS** 2 PERSONS

Ingredients:

- 2 pounds Brussels sprouts
- 2 tablespoons avocado oil
- Salt and pepper, to taste
- 1 cup pine nuts, roasted

Preparations:

1. Trim the bottom of Brussels sprouts.
2. Take a bowl and combine the avocado oil, salt, and black pepper.
3. Toss the Brussels sprouts well.
4. Transfer it to the air fryer basket.
5. Use AIR FRY mode for 20 minutes at 390 degrees F.
6. Once the Brussels sprouts get crisp and tender, take out and serve.

Serving Suggestion: Serve with rice.

Variation Tip: Use olive oil instead of avocado oil.

Nutrition:

CALORIES 672 | FAT 50G | SODIUM 115MG | CARBS 51G | FIBER 20.2G | SUGAR 12.3G | PROTEIN 25G

DESSERTS

APPLE HAND PIES

 **PREPARATION TIME**
15 MINUTES

 **COOKING TIME**
21 MINUTES

 **SERVINGS**
8 PERSONS

Ingredients:

- 8 tablespoons butter, softened
- 12 tablespoons brown sugar
- 2 teaspoons cinnamon, ground
- 4 medium Granny Smith apples, diced
- 2 teaspoons cornstarch
- 4 teaspoons cold water
- 1 (14 oz.) package pastry, 9-inch crust pie
- Cooking spray
- 1 tablespoon grapeseed oil
- ½ cup powdered sugar
- 2 teaspoons milk

Preparations:

1. Preheat your Air Fryer to 390°F using Air Fry mode.
2. Toss apples with brown sugar, butter, and cinnamon in a suitable skillet.
3. Place the skillet over medium heat and stir cook for 5 minutes.
4. Mix cornstarch with cold water in a small bowl.
5. Add cornstarch mixture into the apple and cook for 1 minute until it thickens.
6. Remove this filling from the heat and allow it to cool.
7. Unroll the pie crust and spray on a floured surface.
8. Cut the dough into 16 equal rectangles.
9. Wet the edges of the 8 rectangles with water and divide the apple filling at the center of these rectangles.
10. Place the other 8 rectangles on top and crimp the edges with a fork, then make 2-3 slashes on top.
11. Place the small pies in the Air Fryer Basket.
12. Place the Air Fryer Basket again in the Air Fryer and cook for 17 minutes.
13. Press the START/PAUSE BUTTON to begin cooking.
14. Flip the pies once cooked halfway through, and resume cooking.
15. Meanwhile, mix sugar with milk.
16. Pour this mixture over the apple pies.
17. Serve fresh.

Serving Suggestion: Serve with applesauce.
Variation Tip: Add shredded nuts and coconuts to the filling.

Nutrition:

CALORIES 284 | FAT 16G | SODIUM 252MG | CARBS 31.6G | FIBER 0.9G | SUGAR 6.6G | PROTEIN 3.7G

AIR FRIED BEIGNETS

 **PREPARATION TIME**
15 MINUTES

 COOKING TIME
21 MINUTES

 SERVINGS
6 PERSONS

Ingredients:

- Cooking spray
- ¼ cup white sugar
- ⅛ cup water
- ½ cup all-purpose flour
- 1 large egg, separated
- 1 ½ teaspoons butter, melted
- ½ teaspoon baking powder
- ½ teaspoon vanilla extract
- 1 pinch salt
- 2 tablespoons confectioners' sugar, or to taste

Preparations:

1. Preheat your Air Fryer to 390°F using Air Fry mode.
2. Beat flour with water, sugar, egg yolk, baking powder, butter, vanilla extract, and salt in a large bowl until lumps-free.
3. Beat egg whites in a separate bowl and beat using an electric hand mixer until it forms soft peaks.
4. Add the egg white to the flour batter and mix gently until fully incorporated.
5. Divide the dough into small beignets and place them in the Air Fryer Basket.
6. Place the Air Fryer Basket again in the Air Fryer and cook for 17 minutes.
7. Press the START/PAUSE BUTTON to begin cooking.
8. And cook for another 4 minutes. Dust the cooked beignets with sugar.
9. Serve.

Serving Suggestion: Serve with a dollop of sweet cream dip.

Variation Tip: Add chopped raisins and nuts to the dough.

Nutrition:

CALORIES 327 | FAT 14.2G |SODIUM 672MG | CARBS 47.2G | FIBER 1.7G | SUGAR 24.8G | PROTEIN 4.4G

OREO ROLLS

 **PREPARATION TIME**
10 MINUTES

 COOKING TIME
12 MINUTES

 SERVINGS
9 PERSONS

Ingredients:

- 1 crescent sheet roll
- 9 Oreo cookies
- Cinnamon powder, to serve
- Powdered sugar, to serve

Preparations:

1. Preheat your Air Fryer to 390°F using Air Fry mode.
2. Spread the crescent sheet roll and cut it into 9 equal squares.
3. Place one cookie at the center of each square.
4. Wrap each square around the cookies and press the ends to seal.
5. Place half of the wrapped cookies in the Air Fryer Basket.
6. Place the Air Fryer Basket again in the Air Fryer and cook for 6 minutes.
7. Press the START/PAUSE BUTTON to begin cooking.
8. Cook the remaining cookie rolls in the same way.
9. Garnish the rolls with sugar and cinnamon.
10. Serve.

Serving Suggestion: Serve a cup of spice latte or hot chocolate.

Variation Tip: Dip the rolls in melted chocolate for a change of taste.

Nutrition:

CALORIES 175 | FAT 13.1G |SODIUM 154MG | CARBS 14G | FIBER 0.8G | SUGAR 8.9G | PROTEIN 0.7G

ZESTY CRANBERRY SCONES

PREPARATION TIME
10 MINUTES

COOKING TIME
16 MINUTES

SERVINGS
8 PERSONS

Ingredients:

- 4 cups of flour
- ½ cup brown sugar
- 2 tablespoons baking powder
- ½ teaspoon ground nutmeg
- ½ teaspoon salt
- ½ cup butter, chilled and diced
- 2 cups fresh cranberry
- ⅔ cup sugar
- 2 tablespoons orange zest
- 1 ¼ cups half and half cream
- 2 eggs

Preparations:

1. Preheat your Air Fryer to 390°F using Air Fry mode.
2. Whisk flour with baking powder, salt, nutmeg, and both sugars in a bowl.
3. Stir in egg and cream, mix well to form a smooth dough.
4. Fold in cranberries along with the orange zest.
5. Knead this dough well on a work surface.
6. Cut 3-inch circles out of the dough.
7. Place the scones in the Air Fryer Basket and spray them with cooking oil.
8. Place the Air Fryer Basket again in the Air Fryer and cook for 16 minutes.
9. Press the START/PAUSE BUTTON to begin cooking.
10. Flip the scones once cooked halfway and resume cooking.
11. Enjoy.

Serving Suggestion: Serve with cranberry jam on the side.

Variation Tip: Add raisins instead of cranberries to the dough.

Nutrition:

CALORIES 204 | FAT 9G | SODIUM 91MG | CARBS 27G | FIBER 2.4G | SUGAR 15G | PROTEIN 1.3G

WALNUTS FRITTERS

 **PREPARATION TIME**
15 MINUTES

 **COOKING TIME**
15 MINUTES

 **SERVINGS**
6 PERSONS

Ingredients:

- 1 cup all-purpose flour
- ½ cup walnuts, chopped
- ¼ cup white sugar
- ¼ cup milk
- 1 egg
- 1 ½ teaspoons baking powder
- 1 pinch salt
- Cooking spray
- 2 tablespoons white sugar
- ½ teaspoon ground cinnamon

Glaze:
- ½ cup confectioners' sugar
- 1 tablespoon milk
- ½ teaspoon caramel extract
- ¼ teaspoon ground cinnamon

Preparations:

1. Preheat your Air Fryer to 390°F using Air Fry mode.
2. Layer the Air Fryer Basket with parchment paper.
3. Grease the parchment paper with cooking spray.
4. Whisk flour with milk, ¼ cup of sugar, egg, baking powder, and salt in a small bowl.
5. Separately mix 2 tablespoons of sugar with cinnamon in another bowl, toss in walnuts, and mix well to coat.
6. Stir in flour mixture and mix until combined.
7. Drop the fritters mixture using a cookie scoop into the Air Fryer Basket.
8. Place the Air Fryer Basket again in the Air Fryer and cook for 15 minutes.
9. Press the START/PAUSE BUTTON to begin cooking.
10. Flip the fritters once cooked halfway through, then resume cooking.
11. Meanwhile, whisk milk, caramel extract, confectioners' sugar, and cinnamon in a bowl.
12. Transfer fritters to a wire rack and allow them to cool.
13. Drizzle with a glaze over the fritters.

Serving Suggestion: Serve with butter pecan ice cream or strawberry jam.

Variation Tip: Add maple syrup on top.

Nutrition:

CALORIES 391 | FAT 24G |SODIUM 142MG | CARBS 38.5G | FIBER 3.5G | SUGAR 21G | PROTEIN 6.6G

BISCUIT DOUGHNUTS

 **PREPARATION TIME**
15 MINUTES

 **COOKING TIME**
15 MINUTES

 **SERVINGS**
8 PERSONS

Ingredients:

- ½ cup white sugar
- 1 teaspoon cinnamon
- ½ cup powdered sugar
- 1 can pre-made biscuit dough
- Coconut oil
- Melted butter to brush biscuits

Preparations:

1. Preheat your Air Fryer to 390°F using Air Fry mode.
2. Place all the biscuits on a cutting board and cut holes in the center of each biscuit using a cookie cutter.
3. Grease the Air Fryer Basket with coconut oil.
4. Place the biscuits in the Air Fryer Basket while keeping them 1 inch apart.
5. Place the Air Fryer Basket again in the Air Fryer and cook for 15 minutes.
6. Press the START/PAUSE BUTTON to begin cooking.
7. Brush all the donuts with melted butter and sprinkle cinnamon and sugar on top.
8. Air fry these donuts for one minute more.
9. Enjoy.

Serving Suggestion: Serve the doughnuts with chocolate syrup on top.

Variation Tip: Inject strawberry jam into each doughnut.

Nutrition:

CALORIES 192 | FAT 9.3G | SODIUM 133MG | CARBS 27.1G | FIBER 1.4G | SUGAR 19G | PROTEIN 3.2G

BREAD PUDDING

PREPARATION TIME
12 MINUTES

COOKING TIME
8-12 MINUTES

SERVINGS
2 PERSONS

Ingredients:

- Nonstick spray, for greasing ramekins
- 2 slices white bread, crumbled
- 4 tablespoons white sugar
- 5 large eggs
- ½ cup cream
- Salt, pinch
- ⅓ teaspoon cinnamon powder

Preparations:

1. Whisk eggs to smooth in a bowl
2. Add sugar and salt to the egg and Combine well.
3. Then add cream and use a hand beater to incorporate the entire ingredients.
4. Now add cinnamon, and add crumbs of bread.
5. Mix it well and add it into a round-shaped baking pan.
6. Put it inside the Ninja Air Fryer.
7. Set it on AIR FRY mode at 350 degrees F for 8-12 minutes.
8. Once it's cooked, serve.

Serving Suggestion: Serve it with Coffee.
Variation Tip: Use brown sugar instead of white sugar.

Nutrition:

CALORIES 331 | FAT16.1G | SODIUM 331MG | CARBS 31G | FIBER0.2G | SUGAR 26.2G | PROTEIN 16.2G

PUMPKIN MUFFINS

 **PREPARATION TIME**
20 MINUTES

 **COOKING TIME**
19 MINUTES

 **SERVINGS**
4 PERSONS

Ingredients:

- 1 and ½ cups all-purpose flour
- ½ teaspoon baking soda
- ½ teaspoon of baking powder
- 1 and ¼ teaspoons cinnamon, groaned
- ¼ teaspoon ground nutmeg, grated
- 2 large eggs
- Salt, pinch
- 3/4 cup granulated sugar
- ½ cup dark brown sugar
- 1 and ½ cups of pumpkin puree
- ¼ cup coconut milk

Preparations:

1. Take 4 ramekins that are the size of a cup and layer them with muffin paper.
2. Crack an egg in a bowl and add brown sugar, baking soda, baking powder, cinnamon, nutmeg, and sugar.
3. Whisk it all very well with an electric hand beater.
4. Now, in a second bowl, mix the flour, and salt.
5. Now, mix the dry ingredients slowly with the wet ingredients.
6. Now, at the end fold in the pumpkin puree and milk, mix it well 7. Divide this batter into 4 ramekins.
7. Now, put the ramekins inside the basket.
8. Add the basket to the unit.
9. Set the time to 18 minutes at 360 degrees F at AIR FRY mode.
10. Check if not done, and let it AIR FRY for one more minute.
11. Once it is done, serve.

Serving Suggestion: Serve it with a glass of milk.
Variation Tip: Use almond milk instead of coconut milk.

Nutrition:

CALORIES 291 | FAT6.4 G | SODIUM 241MG | CARBS 57.1G | FIBER 4.4G | SUGAR42 G | PROTEIN 5.9G

LEMONY SWEET TWISTS

 **PREPARATION TIME**
15 MINUTES

 **COOKING TIME**
9 MINUTES

 **SERVINGS**
2 PERSONS

Ingredients:

- 1 box store-bought puff pastry
- ½ teaspoon lemon zest
- 1 tablespoon lemon juice
- 2 teaspoons brown sugar
- Salt, pinch
- 2 tablespoons Parmesan cheese, freshly grated

Preparations:

1. Put the puff pastry dough in a clean work area.
2. In a bowl, combine Parmesan cheese, brown sugar, salt, lemon zest, and lemon juice.
3. Press this mixture on both sides of the dough.
4. Now, cut the pastry into 1" x 4" strips.
5. Twist each of the strips.
6. Transfer it to the air fryer basket.
7. Select the air fry mode at 400 degrees F for 9-10 minutes.
8. Once cooked, serve and enjoy.

Serving Suggestion: Serve it with champagne!
Variation Tip: None.

Nutrition:

CALORIES 156 | FAT 10G | SODIUM 215MG | CARBS 14G | FIBER 0.4G | SUGAR 3.3 G | PROTEIN 2.8G

CHOCOLATE CHIP MUFFINS

 **PREPARATION TIME**
12 MINUTES

 **COOKING TIME**
15 MINUTES

 **SERVINGS**
2 PERSONS

Ingredients:

- Salt, pinch
- 2 eggs
- ⅓ cup brown sugar
- ⅓ cup butter
- 4 tablespoons milk
- ¼ teaspoon vanilla extract
- ½ teaspoon baking powder
- 1 cup all-purpose flour
- 1 pouch chocolate chips, 35 grams

Preparations:

1. Layer muffin papers in four oven-safe ramekins that are the size of a cup.
2. Whisk the egg, brown sugar, butter, milk, and vanilla extract in a mixing dish.
3. Using an electric hand mixer, whisk everything together thoroughly.
4. Combine the flour, baking powder, and salt in a separate bowl.
5. Slowly incorporate the dry components into the wet ingredients.
6. Finally, fold in the chocolate chunks and thoroughly combine them.
7. Pour the batter into four ramekins.
8. Put the ramekins in the basket now.
9. Preheat the oven to 350°F and set the timer for 15 minutes on AIR FRY mode.
10. If it's not done yet, check it and let it AIR FRY for another minute.
11. When it's done, serve

Serving Suggestion: Serve it with chocolate syrup drizzle.

Variation Tip: None.

Nutrition:

CALORIES 757 | FAT40.3G | SODIUM 426MG | CARBS 85.4G | FIBER 2.2G | SUGAR 30.4G | PROTEIN 14.4G

MINI BLUEBERRY PIES

 **PREPARATION TIME**
12 MINUTES

 COOKING TIME
10 MINUTES

 SERVINGS
2 PERSONS

Ingredients:

- 1 box store-bought pie dough, Trader Joe's
- ¼ cup blueberry jam
- 1 teaspoon lemon zest
- 1 egg white, for brushing

Preparations:

1. Cut the 3-inch circles out of the store-bought pie crust.
2. Use an egg white to brush the dough all around the parameters.
3. In the center, spread blueberry jam and zest, then top with another circle.
4. To seal it, use the fork to press the edges together.
5. Cut a slit in the dough in thcenterre and place it in the basket.
6. Preheat the oven to 360°F and cook for 10 minutes on AIR FRY mode.
7. Remove from the oven and serve.

Serving Suggestion: Serve it with vanilla ice cream.
Variation Tip: Use orange zest instead of lemon zest.

Nutrition:

CALORIES 234| FAT 8.6G| SODIUM 187MG | CARBS 38.2 G | FIBER 0.1G | SUGAR13.7 G | PROTEIN 2G

AIR FRIED BANANAS

 **PREPARATION TIME**
10 MINUTES

 **COOKING TIME**
13 MINUTES

 **SERVINGS**
4 PERSONS

Ingredients:

- 4 bananas, sliced
- 1 avocado oil cooking spray

Preparations:

1. At 350 degrees F, preheat your Air Fryer on Air Fry mode.
2. In the Air Fryer Basket, arrange the banana slices in a single layer.
3. Drizzle the banana slices with avocado oil.
4. Return the Air Fryer Basket to the Air Fryer and cook for an additional 13 minutes.
5. To begin cooking, press the START/PAUSE BUTTON.6. Serve.

Serving Suggestion: Serve with a dollop of vanilla ice cream.

Variation Tip: Drizzle chopped nuts on top of the bananas.

Nutrition:

CALORIES 149 | FAT 1.2G |SODIUM 3MG | CARBS 37.6G | FIBER 5.8G | SUGAR 29G | PROTEIN 1.1G

MINI STRAWBERRY AND CREAM PIES

 PREPARATION TIME
12 MINUTES

 COOKING TIME
10 MINUTES

 SERVINGS
2 PERSONS

Ingredients:

- 1 box Store-Bought Pie Dough, Trader Joe's
- 1 cup strawberries, cubed
- 3 tablespoons cream, heavy
- 2 tablespoons almonds
- 1 egg white, for brushing

Preparations:

1. Flatten the store-bought pie crust on a work surface.
2. Cut it into 3-inch circles using a circular cutter.
3. Use an egg white to brush the dough all around the parameters.
4. Place a little amount of almonds, strawberries, and cream in the center of the dough and top with another circle.
5. To seal it, use the fork to press the edges together.
6. Cut a slit in the dough in the center and place it in the basket.
7. Preheat the oven to 350°F and set the timer for 10 minutes on AIR FRY mode.
8. Finally, serve.

Serving Suggestion: Serve it with vanilla ice cream.
Variation Tip: Use orange zest instead of lemon zest.

Nutrition:

CALORIES 203| FAT12.7G| SODIUM 193MG | CARBS20 G | FIBER 2.2G | SUGAR 5.8G | PROTEIN 3.7G

CONCLUSION

With the new Ninja Foodi 2-Basket Air Fryer, cooking any type or size of meal for any time of the day will be easy peasy. This smart 2-Basket air fryer with pace-setting tools is excellently manufactured with a unique dual-zone technology that allows for the cooking of two different meals at once or one large meal using "Smart Finish" or "Match Cooking" technology. Now, life is easier because you can now cook with ease, thanks to Ninja Kitchen.

The dual-zone technology featured in this air fryer is an essential technology that makes cooking a pleasurable experience for everyone. Now, go ahead and try these savory recipes and see how easy they are to cook with your brand new Ninja Foodi 2-Basket Air Fryer.

4 WEEK MEAL PLAN

MEAL PLAN | WEEK 1

MONDAY:
BREAKFAST: BRUSSELS SPROUTS POTATO HASH
LUNCH: HONEY TERIYAKI SALMON
SNACK: BACON WRAPPED TATER TOT
DINNER: THAI CURRY CHICKEN KABOBS
DESSERT: BREAD PUDDING

TUESDAY
BREAKFAST: CHEESY BAKED EGGS
LUNCH: CAJUN SCALLOPS
SNACK: CRISPY POPCORN SHRIMP
DINNER: GREEK CHICKEN MEATBALLS
DESSERT: BAKED APPLES

WEDNESDAY
BREAKFAST: SAUSAGE BREAKFAST CASSEROLE
LUNCH: FURIKAKE SALMON
SNACK: AVOCADO FRIES WITH SRIRACHA DIP
DINNER: CHICKEN CAPRESE
DESSERT: BLUEBERRY PIE EGG ROLLS

THURSDAY
BREAKFAST: ROASTED ORANGES
LUNCH: TUNA STEAKS
SNACK: ONION RINGS
DINNER: CORNISH HEN
DESSERT: STRAWBERRY SHORTCAKE

FRIDAY
BREAKFAST: BREAKFAST FRITTATA
LUNCH: SHRIMP WITH LEMON AND PEPPER
SNACK: POTATO CHIPS
DINNER: TERIYAKI CHICKEN SKEWERS
DESSERT: DESSERT EMPANADAS

SATURDAY
BREAKFAST: JELLY DOUGHNUTS
LUNCH: STUFFED MUSHROOMS WITH CRAB
SNACK: CRAB CAKES
DINNER: CHICKEN KEBABS
DESSERT: MONKEY BREAD

SUNDAY
BREAKFAST: APPLE FRITTERS
LUNCH: FOIL PACKET SALMON
SNACK: FRIED RAVIOLI
DINNER: JUICY DUCK BREAST
DESSERT: GRILLED PEACHES

MEAL PLAN | WEEK 2

MONDAY:
BREAKFAST: BREAKFAST STUFFED PEPPERS
LUNCH: AIR FRYER CALAMARI
SNACK: FRIED CHEESE
DINNER: CRISPY FRIED QUAIL
DESSERT: BREAD PUDDING

TUESDAY
BREAKFAST: BREAKFAST POTATOES
LUNCH: HONEY PECAN SHRIMP
SNACK: CINNAMON SUGAR CHICKPEAS
DINNER: ASIAN PORK SKEWERS
DESSERT: CINNAMON BREAD TWISTS

WEDNESDAY
BREAKFAST: CORNBREAD
LUNCH: CRUMB-TOPPED SOLE
SNACK: ONION RINGS

DINNER: BEEF KOFTA KEBAB

DESSERT: VICTORIA SPONGE CAKE

THURSDAY

BREAKFAST: BRUSSELS SPROUTS POTATO HASH

LUNCH: PRETZEL-CRUSTED CATFISH

SNACK: BACON WRAPPED TATER TOT

DINNER: BEEF KABOBS

DESSERT: DESSERT EMPANADAS

FRIDAY

BREAKFAST: CHEESY BAKED EGGS

LUNCH: BROWN SUGAR GARLIC SALMON

SNACK: CRISPY POPCORN SHRIMP

DINNER: STEAK AND ASPARAGUS BUNDLES

DESSERT: BLUEBERRY PIE EGG ROLLS

SATURDAY

BREAKFAST: SAUSAGE BREAKFAST CASSEROLE

LUNCH: CHILI LIME TILAPIA

SNACK: AVOCADO FRIES WITH SRIRACHA DIP

DINNER: CHEESESTEAK TAQUITOS

DESSERT: BAKED APPLES

SUNDAY

BREAKFAST: ROASTED ORANGES

LUNCH: CRISPY PARMESAN COD

SNACK: ONION RINGS

DINNER: AIR FRIED LAMB CHOPS

DESSERT: BLUEBERRY PIE EGG ROLLS

MEAL PLAN | WEEK 3

MONDAY:

BREAKFAST: BREAKFAST FRITTATA

LUNCH: BACON WRAPPED STUFFED CHICKEN

SNACK: POTATO CHIPS

DINNER: BBQ PORK CHOPS

DESSERT: STRAWBERRY SHORTCAKE

TUESDAY

BREAKFAST: JELLY DOUGHNUTS

LUNCH: PRETZEL CHICKEN CORDON BLEU

SNACK: CRAB CAKES

DINNER: PORK CHOPS WITH APPLES

DESSERT: DESSERT EMPANADAS

WEDNESDAY

BREAKFAST: APPLE FRITTERS

LUNCH: CHICKEN AND POTATOES

SNACK: FRIED RAVIOLI

DINNER: CINNAMON-APPLE PORK CHOPS

DESSERT: MONKEY BREAD

THURSDAY

BREAKFAST: BREAKFAST STUFFED PEPPERS

LUNCH: CRISPY SESAME CHICKEN

SNACK: FRIED CHEESE

DINNER: BACON WRAPPED PORK TENDERLOIN

DESSERT: GRILLED PEACHES

FRIDAY

BREAKFAST: BREAKFAST POTATOES LUNCH: JAMAICAN FRIED CHICKEN

SNACK: CINNAMON SUGAR CHICKPEAS

DINNER: STEAK BITES WITH COWBOY BUTTER

DESSERT: CINNAMON BREAD TWISTS

SATURDAY

BREAKFAST: CORNBREAD

LUNCH: AIR FRIED CHICKEN LEGS

SNACK: BACON WRAPPED TATER TOT

DINNER: AIR FRIED LAMB CHOPS

DESSERT: VICTORIA SPONGE CAKE

SUNDAY

BREAKFAST: ROASTED ORANGES

LUNCH: CRISPY PARMESAN COD

SNACK: ONION RINGS

DINNER: AIR FRIED LAMB CHOPS

DESSERT: BLUEBERRY PIE EGG ROLLS

MONDAY:
BREAKFAST: BRUSSELS SPROUTS POTATO HASH
LUNCH: HONEY TERIYAKI SALMON
SNACK: BACON WRAPPED TATER TOT
DINNER: THAI CURRY CHICKEN KABOBS
DESSERT: BREAD PUDDING

TUESDAY
BREAKFAST: CHEESY BAKED EGGS
LUNCH: CAJUN SCALLOPS
SNACK: CRISPY POPCORN SHRIMP
DINNER: GREEK CHICKEN MEATBALLS
DESSERT: BAKED APPLES

WEDNESDAY
BREAKFAST: SAUSAGE BREAKFAST CASSEROLE
LUNCH: FURIKAKE SALMON
SNACK: AVOCADO FRIES WITH SRIRACHA DIP
DINNER: CHICKEN CAPRESE
DESSERT: BLUEBERRY PIE EGG ROLLS

THURSDAY
BREAKFAST: ROASTED ORANGES
LUNCH: TUNA STEAKS
SNACK: ONION RINGS
DINNER: CORNISH HEN
DESSERT: STRAWBERRY SHORTCAKE

FRIDAY
BREAKFAST: BREAKFAST FRITTATA LUNCH: SHRIMP
WITH LEMON AND PEPPER
SNACK: POTATO CHIPS
DINNER: TERIYAKI CHICKEN SKEWERS
DESSERT: DESSERT EMPANADAS

SATURDAY
BREAKFAST: JELLY DOUGHNUTS
LUNCH: STUFFED MUSHROOMS WITH CRAB
SNACK: CRAB CAKES
DINNER: CHICKEN KEBABS
DESSERT: MONKEY BREAD

SUNDAY
BREAKFAST: APPLE FRITTERS
LUNCH: FOIL PACKET SALMON
SNACK: FRIED RAVIOLI
DINNER: JUICY DUCK BREAST
DESSERT: GRILLED PEACHES

INDEX

Printed in Great Britain
by Amazon